The Treason of the Intellectuals

and other political verse

Sean Matgamna

In memory of Minnie Cleary, of Milltown, Ennis, and Manchester, 1903 to September 1974; and Tommy Mahony, of Ennis, Birmingham, and Manchester, 1906 to November 1974.

Lulu Press 2012
ISBN 978-1-4710-1096-5

Cover picture: members of the Ennis United Labourers' Union, on relief work breaking stones by hand, in about 1938. They are sitting on a pile of stones, at the side of a country road. Front line, second from left (facing camera) is "Neiber" Molloy. Second on right, Tommy Mahony, a defendant in the 1934 trial of 24 Ennis labourers for mass picketing and the author's father. Back row, first on right facing the camera, maybe, Jack Moloney, also a defendant in the 1934 trial; second from left facing camera, maybe, John Frawley. Photographer unknown.

Introduction

I have, I suppose, a sneaky hope for a few of these pieces, but in general I make no claim that this is poetry. That belongs to a higher order of things. This is workaday political verse – politics in its broad social sense, including the politics of such things as religion and mass emigration from Ireland. It is the sort of verse that was once very common in socialist and other publications and is now rare. All questions of quality aside, these pieces belong to the sort of verse I encountered as a child in Ireland.

The politics here is working-class revolutionary socialism, in the tradition of the "thin red line" of international socialist resistance to both Stalinism and the bourgeoisie, in all their many political guises. That line runs unbroken through all the catastrophes of defeat and self-transformation that engulfed 20th century socialism.

Some of these pieces explore feelings, unfiltered moods, and political nuance; some are self-questioning. Many of them date from the time when Russian and East European Stalinism was collapsing. People of my politics had ardently wanted that, but now Stalinism gave way not, as we had hoped and believed it would, to a new working class socialism but to a re-born capitalism.

The same sort of political self-questioning, edged in painful disappointment and sometimes in guilt, went through the minds of many socialists then in a spiritual-political crisis. One of the advantages of verse is that it lends itself easily to the sifting of such things. Nonetheless, bits of one-sided insomniac's verse are not rounded political statements. My straightforward political response to these events appeared in articles, of which there were quite a few, in the weekly *Socialist Organiser*, and in the magazine *Workers' Liberty*.

Political verse nowadays tends to be dismissed as a contradiction in terms. I can't see why politics, and to the point with many of these pieces, the emotional, personal experience of political events, is not a perfectly proper subject for verse (and, if one could manage that, for poetry itself).

Many of these pieces were published in *Socialist Organiser*, *Workers' Liberty* and *Solidarity*. Some have been published on the Workers' Liberty website, www.workersliberty.org. The reader interested in situating the pieces in the time they were published or written will find a list of dates and approximate dates at the back of the book.

Sean Matgamna, 1-1-2012.

The Treason of the Intellectuals

Bookless, you have the one sweet narrow time,
Can know only your own brief hungry place,
Live in a dark slow-burning carapace
A wild, raw-minded, unexamined mime.
The book-rich too are held in time's tight rime
To one-beat sentience, yet may embrace
Wide times and distant living, know the race,
See out beyond the banked effluvial grime.
So schooled folk say, with pride. Then tell me why,
In every age and place, the book-proud clerk
Colludes to rob and pen in the lightless sty
Millions condemned to half-life in the dark?
As dog to primal hunter, clerk to chief:
Fawning, he stalks, then guzzles, with the thief!

Remember!

Remember me, and hold you strait within
Your mind and soul, though others slink and swerve;
Remember then, when fear did not unnerve
High hope, before the apostate's tide came in;
Remember, now, the Beauty of the days
That lit your morning eyes, gave sense to Time
When you were new: remember! In your prime
Tend youth-set Truth, though others douse the blaze.
Let come what comes, hold to what you then wove
Of the splendid world, serve still with Hope and Will
The angry, glowing aisling* no-one can kill:
Life that is ruled by reason fraught with love,
Where now Hate rules, and Truth, afraid to brave
Despair, lurks by the stark precocious grave.

*An aisling is an Irish "vision poem".

Karl Marx in August

(To the tune of "Joe Hill")
I dreamt I saw Karl Marx last night,
I saw him standing there,
His hair jet black, no longer white,
Fierce eyes, and a bold young stare:
His eyes had a young man's stare.

I saw Marx youthful, angry there,
I said in my surprise:
"But you grew old, white beard and hair…"
And then Marx cried: "All lies!"
And then Marx cried: " — Damn lies!"

"A ghost to comfort those who'd lost
Their spark, themselves half dead;
They made me old, grey with disgust
— I'm young again!" he said,
"I'm young again," he said.

"Alive again! You see I'm back,
My spirit never fled,
I'm young, bold, vigorous, black:
I'm me again", he said.
I'm me again!", he said.

I dreamt I saw Karl Marx last night,
He stood before me there,
His hair jet black, no longer white,
Fierce eyes, with a young man's stare,
Fierce eyes and a bold young stare.

The Russian Stalinist empire collapsed in August 1991

In Assisi

Midst the avarice and sanctity
In Assisi, white in sun and years,
Two flushed, pale-bloused, young-breasted girls,
Their mouths half-open, smiling, watch
Two pigeons fucking in the sun.

Breath held in Francis-empathy,
Delighted, knowing hands entwined,
Unconsciously at one, they catch
Life fired by the pantheistic sun.

And then, their eyes cloud and drop,
As the shade-faced, fussing shepherd nun
Comes at a dry stiff trot — cast down
Like the dead saint's communistic friends
Who broke the sacerdotal line,
To set life over property.

They burned in priest-set fires, whose minds
Too soon had seen a precious sight:
Who saw as true as the children see
These pigeons loving in the light.

St Francis of Assisi, who might be describes as a pantheistic primitive communist, preached, in the early 13th century, poverty, the community of all life and the love of all living things, Divesting himself of property, he aligned himself with the poor. Some of his co-thinkers who refused to soften the ideas they had shared with Francis, ideas which might have been developed in the direction of revolutionary social conclusions, were persecuted as heretics. Franciscan friars are today a strong, world-wide Catholic religious order.

And where were Jacob Sverdlov's sons?

Sverdlov killed the bloody Tsar,
He signed the warrant for it;
So when they struck his statue down
The Tsarists cheered who saw it:
They hauled the hollow statue down,
And the Tsarists sang when they saw it.

And where were Jacob Sverdlov's sons?
And Lenin's proud granddaughters?
And where were Trotsky's Bolsheviks?
All of them lost, slaughtered;
All of the leaders, fighters, Reds,
All of them, all, slaughtered!

They made no statues out of bronze,
The heroes Stalin killed;
In Lubianka and Vorkuta
They died, their voices stilled:
The Tsar's song fills the air this dawn
Because their voice was stilled.

They died defending working folk,
And who now cares to tell
Their tale, recall the fight of those
Old Communists who fell?
With lies they've sealed the graves of those
Old Communists, too well.

When tsarists sing the Tsar's old song
And Socialism's worth a sneer,
Who cares for the Reds that Stalin killed?
Dim pictures from afar
Of the tribe wiped out to clear the way
For those who hail the Tsar.

And where were Jacob Sverdlov's sons,
And Trotsky's armed granddaughters?
And where were Lenin's Bolsheviks?
All of them, all, slaughtered;
All of the leaders, fighters, Reds,
All of them, all, slaughtered!

"The Trots"

Spending our lives in outcasts' work,
We are "The Trots" — and we still lurk
For all that History could wreak:
The key to higher times we seek,
To the remade world that proves elusive,
Although capitalism moles still, conducive
To our desire, whose fires it set:
In us, a class refuses to forget!

Phoenix!

I am the Phoenix
I will not die!
I have been drowned in fire and blood
By open foes, devoured
By predatory allies and masters; reduced,
I rise again:
I saw Hitler loom above Rosa Luxemburg's grave
And then fled East
To hail his other self
I am the true Phoenix.

I hailed Stalin
Saviour and Father of the Peoples
The no-Tsar, Tsar,
The Peoples' own Red King
A comrade, dialecticked,
Though Stalin had built himself a mausoleum
To strut on in triumph, dancing
On the poor dry bones and waxy blind
Forever silent ruin
Of the dead iconoclast Vladimir Lenin
I am the Phoenix.

I saw Mao
And Mao's Red peasant army moving through
Shanghai's old streets
Where Chiang had butchered
Riding in triumph
To the palaces of my murderers
And I hailed Mao as God

My all-renewing saviour
I am the Phoenix
I never die.

I fall in love with monsters
I cross-bred with horror
My children were all monsters, or died young
Many are born dead
But I make life: I go on
I am the Phoenix.

I am ignorant, credulous
Senseless, wayward, often fooled: often fooled
But I live
And I will not die!
I torment seduce cajole rouse energise mesmerise
I am treacherous delusive self-deluding
Rest-destroying, death defying
Id-sprung, I make life!
I am the Phoenix.

I am the heart of heartless worlds
The sigh of the oppressed in vales of woe
Guileless, I have searched the Twentieth Century
For my fatherland
I have searched amongst verminous cults
For the cult, the saviour
That is not verminous
That saves. I have proved Carlyle right
It was a choice of an elite
And yet I live, reborn.
I am prolific
I rise and go down, sometimes in blood

And yet I rise again and again and again
I am the Phoenix.
I will not die.

I am Caliban
Caliban overthrown, enslaved
Who would be mine own king again
I choose a shipwrecked drunken sailor on a beach
To be my saviour and my king, if he
Will kill oppressive Prospero.
I am the serf who prays to the Devil
To the enemy of my enemy's God.
I can not die. I go on.
I am the Phoenix.

I was in that grey old bearded man
Who knew relentless death stalking him close
Had claimed his children
And all his tribe.
He made me from green and sunlit grass
Beneath a window
And from blue sky
High above a Mexican wall
Proclaiming I should live
Though he was certain soon to die.
I give life. I am life.
Id-rooted, I
I am the Phoenix
I will not die!

Workers will fight to live
To be their own king:
To give relinquish suffer fight

Knowing yourself a slave
You must know more than yourself
Or you will know less: I am more
Though often, often, I am less!
I am the Phoenix.

I have seen Spartacus crucified
Ten thousand times
And then ten thousand times
And still I live; reborn
I rise up out of the foaming blood, proclaiming
With Rosa, out from the Kaiser Wilhelm's jail
And on the eve of defeat and death:
I was. I am. I will be.
I will be because I must be.
I am the Phoenix
I give life,
I will not die.

I am hope, Proletarian hope.

I learn to see. I can see what lies behind,
But I am born, and reborn, always, blind.

Left-wing anti-semite

Why do you misconstrue my view?
Believe me, I don't hate no Jew;
And seeing what pure love will do,
What need have I for hatred too?

We learn to fly

Lenin and Trotsky lost; defeated, they died.
You tell me: "They could not have ever won,
Those blood-infected dreamers, who essayed
So much, hubristic in their raw Red pride,
To leave a world dismayed, worse disarrayed:
Nothing can rise, once thus self-crucified!"
Daedalus dares, and Icarus will die:
And yet, to spite harsh Gods, we learn— we fly!

In the legend, Daedalus made wings for his son Icarus; but Icarus flew
up too high above the earth, and too near to the sun, until the wax
binding his wings melted, and he crashed to his death.

An Island for Citizen Procrustes

It happens often: "You?" (They mean to cut.)
"No Irishman!" My politics don't fit;
The island is the nation: not "them", "it."
Folk? No — lake, plain and rock! But you must not
Arraign these dancers of the communal strut,
Or wash old blood out of your eyes, or audit
The soundings from the suppurating pit,
Or look to Tone — dry bones, stomped underfoot.
"West Brit: not your identity or birth
Or inbred love of the Gael tells who you are
Or names your place: strait politics en-girth
In-gather: we define, and we debar!"
The real is cut to fit a false design
Grown monstrously unreal, then malign.

In the old Greek tale, Procrustes, a crazy innkeeper, murdered his
lodgers trying to fit them exactly to his beds. The short he stretched
on a rack to elongate them; the tall he chopped down to his preferred
size, ripping off feet or head.

Sunday before war

Whitechapel, East London, January 13 1991

Rattling, clatt'ring, reverberating echoes roar
And bounce along the streets outside the hospital,
Big swirling blades appear upon its high flat brow
Above Whitechapel Road this cold bright Sunday
    morning,
Engines of mercy test their wings for war:
Helicopters are on the roof, rehearsing, warning!
See the maimed, the coffined, blind and mad returning:
Helicopters are on the roof, rehearsing— warning!

Below, a sleek content street-trading man
Lays out fresh flowers for the visiting hour.
Soon oil-fields, cities, seas, and babies will be burning:
Helicopters are on the roof, rehearsing— warning!

The gilded white-walled mosque is sullen, scorning
Fixed in the skein, weighing loss with gain,
Out-shouted by the chattering blades that fly;
Arcane, well-muffled Bangladeshis hurry by.
And suspect alien brown-skinned men scorning
Helicopters are on the roof, rehearsing— warning!

From the car park market gleaning what they can
Two well-dressed women hurry to the tube
Humping high-back kitchen chairs home to the nest:
Is it the cold, or are others too distressed?
See the maimed, the coffined, blind and mad returning:

Helicopters are on the roof, rehearsing— warning!

Behind mad ripper Jack's wrecked lanes they sell:
Here, staking out their place in the market Arcadia,
Ragged men lay trash for sale down on footpaths,
Bare stalls sell rusted tools, old clothes, old nails;
Junk they sell from old folk's lairs, bequest
Of wealth from those despoiled and dispossessed,
Last riches from the life-long near-distressed,
All teapots, vinyl, lamps, big radios, dust-scored,
Lives rendered down, spread out on broken boards.
See the maimed, the coffined, blind and mad returning:
Helicopters are on the roof, rehearsing— warning!

Wholly dispossessed, the lost, mad, ruined
Drunkards shelter by the station— junked freight,
Obsolete! There, neat on a vendor's stall, stacked hate
Filled jingo prints, flash-portraits of a wounded
Bourgeois soul: its parody— its aureole!
And high above the whoring propagandists cold
    suborning
Helicopters are on the roof, rehearsing, warning

On Whitechapel Road this frost-bright Sunday morning
Cold, covened drunks look up on spinning blades
And see the high, big, noisy renegade
Engines of mercy test their wings for war:
Late Mercy for their own; mercy after, not before.
Helicopters are on the roof, rehearsing— warning!
Soon oilfields, cities, seas and babies will be burning:
Helicopters are on the roof, rehearsing — warning!

Soon oil-fields, cities, seas and babies will be burning;

See the maimed, the coffined, blind and mad returning:
Helicopters are on the roof, rehearsing— warning!

Prague, November '89

"It's a pity I'm so old", the woman said,
"But still I'm glad. Oh, I'm glad, I'm glad!"
And sad, like one who knows she'll soon be dead.
In fifty years but three such Springs she's had,
And all her adult life was spent in bondage,
To Hitler, then to Stalin, then to Stalin's
Brute, enfeebled heirs in brigandage;
And now she's old and ending, life begins!
Old worker in our "workers' state", who never
Knew that we approved (reluctantly)
And maybe never cared quite what the answer
Was, about their place in history.
In Prague, November nineteen eighty nine,
When Stalin's heirs had reached the end of the line.

Aul' Mill Street, Ennis

(Tommy Mahony's song)

The jetsam with the flotsam off the land,
Uprooted, displaced people, we make do
The best we can: "No stake in the country, you!"
Settled tinkers! Day labour at command
To anyone with money in his hand;
Drovers and scollop-cutting brawlers who
Half-starve — "Tis Ireland will be free, not you!"
We wear in this farmer's town the weasel's brand.
Unlettered gaums we are, to pluck and fleece
Or export on the hoof, alongside cattle,
To factory and battlefield — wild geese
Who fledge then flee to Salford and Seattle.
And still I feel beneath my fugitive feet
The anger roaring down through Aul' Mill Street!

Old Mill Street, and its continuation Cloughleigh, was one of a
number of long streets of one-storey working class houses stretching
to the west of the town of Ennis. The others were The Turnpike and
Drumbiggle. The great-grandfather of Mohammed Ali, Abe Grady,
migrated from Drumbiggle.
Scollops were long hazel saplings, cut and sold for use in thatching.

An old docker reflects on his fate

I'll soon be white as cold set wax
A dead old red vaquero,
Because I went on Salford Docks
To fight beside the heroes.

A world in flux, and I was young,
Our strikes a fitful gale,
The old *Red Flag* the song we sung:
We knew we would prevail.

And soon I'll go, close the book,
Asbestos did for me
I breathed when I plied the hook
And fought to set us free.

I could have gone to get my cards.
In servile war asbestos
In your lungs was "personal" – hard:
To shirk, impossible loss.

I did not flinch, I did not hedge,
A mountainy, stark youth,
I ate the Salmon of Knowledge
And faced the acrid truth:

Life poisoned by wage slavery,
My mother "bore me in bondage",
In bondage she was born, unfree

In their free Ireland. The age

Long rage for nation-building broke
One chain, cut the spancel
With England, but left the oaken yoke
For workers still to cancel.

And we must serve our own raw need,
Secure our children's lives
By servicing relentless greed
For money, sharp as knives.

"My fathers served their fathers", thus
Since before Moses lied
And since before great Spartacus
Was tied and crucified.

I knew, could make no sense of life,
Or find my place in it,
Except revolt, class war, red strife:
By this my way was lit.

I worked to down wage-slavers' laws,
To end industrial serfdom,
I served the blood-Red ancient cause:
I fought for human freedom!

"And some unknown, unfriended fell
Within the dungeons gloom",
In England's jails, in Stalin's hell.
Amen, to this my doom.

I fought the prole's prolonged long fight,

Rough History's decree:
The wage slaves' red prescient fight,
That proves we will be free!

I stirred the fire, I held the light.

Politics?

"Politics"? Talking out
Of both sides of your mouth,
Reining in, when you want
To shout and jeer and taunt;
Saying half, or less,
Meaning "No", mouthing "Yes":
There everything is tact,
Ideas artefact;
Obtuseness, muddle, fudge:
The greatest crime to judge
Or try to think things through,
To tell plain truths – say "Boo!"
Dare to! Diplomacy,
Is all that here is free!
Where everything is tact
You need a Clean Air Act.
Give me knives, guns, half-bricks,
But give me Lenin's politics!

After an evening spent negotiating with Labour Party Marxists gone
native.

Trotsky and Time

Pinioned by History's revenging lie,
"Life can be free and fine", old Pero said,
And Koba split his stubborn high old head,
Pulled by the weighted years back to comply,
Back through time's dense coils, he dared contest,
To where the King-priest Moctezuma bled;
While masked-up Koba peonised workers, fed
His blind, blood-wet, heart-ripping, Lie-bred quest.
Time tells, retracts, enweaves, can multiply:
Cortez crossed Time's life-sedimented sea
Millennia, back to the pharaohs. Pero? He
Spurred cyclone Time; 'till Time fell all awry.
Back-sailing pirates loot Time's stored reward:
Liberty's pilgrims forge their own gold hoard.

Leon Trotsky died on 21 August 1940. Pero, "the Pen", was a
pseudonym used by the young Trotsky. Koba was Stalin's nickname to
his old Georgian comrades.

This is dystopia, lady!

What world is this, sir?
This is *Dystopia*, lady!
World of hallucogenic sights
And waking nightmares;
Realm of Dire Remembrances
And of things seen in our Bleak Imaginings.

Strange ancient worlds still are threaded in
This ending-time of mankind's long pre-history:
See it through the lenses of its parts,
Its smaller, true and fancied,
Past and present, parts,
And of its pasts,
If you would see it plain,
And know what centuries this is:
Here old and new combine;
Progress and regress intertwine.

II
This is the *Great Dalek Civilisation,*
Run by little shrivelled, dishrag things, strutting
Inside a big, relentless blind machine.

This is the *Western Town*
In the cowboy picture: robbers rule here,
The sheriff and the hangman work for them;
Crooks make and break the Law.

This is the village in the *"Seven Samurai":*
Bandits force tribute

From starved and half-starved people,
Indifferent to the hunger cries.

Here, the educated, knowing, clever
Thinkers, teachers, writers, philosophers,
Pundits, seers, prophets,
Humanity's effete recusant elite,
Gang with the bandits
To rob the hungry villagers:
To the bandits' primal theft and force
They add their own anointing weasel cries.

III
Here, *Freedom and Equality* thrive:
The poor as well as the rich are free
To sleep out in winter city streets.

All alike are barred by law
From robbing banks,
Save only those with wealth enough
To pay the licence fee
For stark impunity,
To loot and rob within the Law.

Those who rob banks with guns are jailed;
Those who use banks like guns
To rob and ride the people, rule
The jails, the Cortes, Senates, Commons,
Assemblies, Reichstags, Dumas, Knessets, Dails.

New little thieves are jailed
Or have their hands cut off
By the Thieves Who Rule

Heir to the greater thieves of old,

IV
This is a place that *Thomas More*,
Lord Chancellor of England knew:
Government is a "perpetual conspiracy
Of the rich against the poor".
This is *Imperial Rome*:
Here, the *Presidency of the World*
Is sought and sold and bought, auctioned,
And, four years on, is sold again,
Democratically by the very rich,
To the very rich, for the very rich.

This is a *Henry Ford Democracy*:
You can choose the colour of your rulers,
Provided it is a shade of the colour bourgeois.

This is a world ruled by *Public Opinion*,
Where Public Opinion is ruled by venal
Journo servitors of the ruling rich.

V
Lady, this is the place of *Swift's imagining*,
Babies, millions from every crop,
Are staked out on the unhealing,
Unsustaining, stark, barren rock, die
To feed the Lords of Money, Law and Life.

Ours, is a world rich
In its *Doctors Mengele*,
Experimenting endlessly,
Generation upon generation,

To find how much
In food and medics' care
Children can lack, and live.

Here, Citizens *Procrustes* and *Moreau*
Run the schools: children are maimed,
Have hopes, propensities, aspirings
Hacked away,
As once they broke the limbs of beggar kids
And re-set them, all awry;
Are shaped and schooled
To make them fit to live
In their allotted place,
To fill and till their social slot
And let their lives be filched
By the ruling lout elite

Lady, this is *Bram Stoker Territory:*
Here, if they can, they drink your blood.

VI
Here, *God* serves *Satan:*
The priests of the high Morality go in lockstep
With the brigands, hangmen, bagmen, murderers and
  Thieves.

Commerce and its Conveniences,
Are fountain alike
Of Law, Morality, Art;
The Stockholder, his priest,
Lawyer, spin-liar,
And his hacking journalist,
Are Moses, Marx, Mohammed, Christ.

The *Money-Changers* own the *Temples*:
Usurer-scourging Jesus is jailed
As a hooligan, and crucified
For lèse Majesty, and lèse God.

Not "Do to others as you
Would have them do to you",
But "do them as they
Might do you, and do it first".

Thievery, robbery, chicanery,
Grown old and numbingly familiar,
Nest deep within the social seed:
Few now will call the Great Thieves, "thieves"
Or name Big Thievery, "theft".

Falling fine acidic rain,
The moral culture eats
At the ties and fabrics of the society
That makes, remakes, sustains and poisons it.

VII
Lady, this is a world ruled-over,
By *Conquistadors*:
Entrenched, still looting predatory victors,
And their victims, vanquished
In savage old class wars,
That change in form, but do not cease:
A war of social worlds rips and rages.

This is the world of *Spartacus*:
Freedom and slavery entwine, symbiotic still;
The pitiless chains,

Longer now, and less visible,
Are forged and reforged, relentlessly.

The means of life,
The work of nature,
And of the generations,
Are held by a few,
Run by mercenaries,
Guarded by scribblers, lawyers, prattlers, cops:
The rest must pay eternal dues
To the Lords of Life, who make the Law.

You must work, wage slave,
Unpaid for part of each long day
For masters of land, bank, plant,
Or they won't let you work at all.

Most hire out their labour power,
A few sell body parts outright,
Many sell their own starved blood.

Here they treat most of the people
Most of the time
As farmers treat their beasts.

This is the *Theatre of the Absurd*:
Here the rich and their ticket-touts
Have pre-booked all the good surveying seats.

This is the *land in the cowboy picture*
Held by the half-mad cattle baron
Against diggers of the soil
And their need

To grow food and people.

This is the world of the *lotus-eaters*,
The Realm of Amnesia:
Here you are induced to forget
Who you are, and what,
And what you and yours might be.

Humankind is snared
In a world-enmeshing web
By the busy, spid'ring bourgeoisie:
Lives are drained, reduced, shrivelled,
Made senselessly arid, emptied, blind.

This is the planet in *Star Trek*
Ruled by *Doctor Frankenstein*,
Here, they steal your kidneys,
Your hands, your eyes, your heart,
For spare part surgery on prospered citizens.

VIII
Here we pray to *The Three Malignant Gods*,
Hope-of-Wealth, Wealth, Profit,
And Their anointed Saints and Holy Souls,
In whom the quest for wealth
Ended with their birth.

Here footballers and singers
Athletes, musicians, models,
Disc-jockeys, psychics, gurus
Our spiritual out-reach; our epitome,
Are adored and tithed.

Here live olympian *Hero-Drones*
Of *conspicuous consumption*
And their attendant swarms
Of addled *Cargo Cultists*.*

Here, too, reign *Pearly Kings and Queens*;
Shimmering tinsel is worn,
Not with shame but pride:
The cherished wealth is glittering nothingness.

A Princess Di is Queen of Hearts,
A Paris Hilton Queen of Heaven
To mesmer'ed, would-be clones
Who browse, voyeur, gawp, gasp, eternally
Wishing, hoping, lusting, longing,
Imagining, miming: helpless
Before the *Great Shop Window*
And its mincing manikins.

IX.
This is the world and this the Age
Of humankind's *Great Fear*,
Of immanent, close-crowding doom
And all-pervading guilt;
The dawning, gnawing sense,
That humankind has fouled its nest;
An Age of surging, burgeoning Fear
Before the looming shadow
Of the Tsunami Times coming;
Engulfing tidal nature waves,
And waves of man-made social devastation.

This is an *Aztec* world, Lady,

Moored and mired in blood-drenched Faith:
Here beating human hearts
Are ripped out of the living flesh,
And sacrificed to the ravening *Market-God,*
Without whose favour nothing moves.

Humanity's heavy-dragging tail
Rises up, again, and again, to strike
At our all too-slow-advancing head.

This is the world of *The Big Sleep*:
Of murk, enshrouding fog,
And deep, self-multiplying mystery:
Even the authors lose the shape of this mad tale!

X
This, Lady, is *Caveman Planet*:
Here bones and toxic dung and dirt
Pile up over the years; except,
We have no other cave to move on to.

And this... Lady... This is...

Sir, it is all these things, you say,
Metaphorically – but what is it,
Beyond analogue and metaphor?

Why, Capitalism, Lady, *Capitalism!*

This is a state of society
In which the process of production
Has the mastery over humankind
Instead of being controlled by us.

Relentless mills of commerce grind:
In a world of finite things,
In-built, *Incessant Waste*
And pre-set built-in early obsolescence,
The ruin-price we pay
Our all-devouring, all-deciding,
Humankind-deriding
Paramount God: Profit.

Lady, this is *Animal Farm*:
The pigs rule here!

But, sir, will things always, here, be so?

No, lady. No. Hell, no!

And, sir, what should I do in Dystopia?

*Cargo Cult: during World War 2, the setting up of a US South Sea
island base, kept in supplies by aeroplanes, produced amongst the
stone-age level native people of the island a cult of the cargo.
Supernatural, the planes disgorging their wonders seemed to them;
and so they ceased economic activity and instead took to aping the
behaviour of the in-comers and praying and sacrificing to the God of
Airborne Supplies, looking for the magic that would bring cargoes to
them too... There is now a large strain in evangelical Christianity —
which elevates emotion and wishful thinking above any form of
rational appraisal of reality — that has been justly branded a species
of cargo-cultism. This is "prosperity preaching", in which Christianity
is "sold" as bringing with it, if only you believe fervently enough,
financial rewards. It is especially strong in Nigeria.

October 1917

Who fears to praise Red Seventeen?
Who quails at Lenin's name?
When liars jeer at Trotsky's fate
Who adds his, "Theirs the blame"?

Cain-Stalin's slave, or bourgeois brave
Will scorn the Old Cause thus,
But honest men and women
Will raise a voice with us.

We praise the memory of the dead,
Of Lenin's friends long gone
Who led the workers in revolt:
An army, not a throng.

All, all are gone, but still lives on
The cause of those who died
And honest men and women
Remember them with pride.

They rose in blood drenched, war-burn'd days
To help set workers free
Their own lives fed the living blaze
That challenged tyranny.

But bourgeois might half-vanquished right
Some fell in disarray,
And others spun 'neath Stalin s gun
— And we strive still today!

We work to free all those who live
In bourgeois slavery
And glory in the names of those
Who fought for Liberty.

'Trenched bourgeois might won't vanquish right
But break and go astray.
And honest men and women
Will speed them on their way!

Yes, we dare praise Red Seventeen,
We honour Lenin's name.
Though cowards mock the old Red fight,
We're still in Trotsky's game!
Though Stalin's knaves and bourgeois slaves
Must scorn the Old Cause thus,
Still honest men and women
Will voice this faith with us.

We hail the memory of the free,
Of Trotsky's 'durate few
Who fought in France, Spain, Germany,
In Stalin's Russia too.
Though all are gone, they still live on,
Their cause won't go away
And honest men and women
Can sing their song today.

Then here's their memory, may it be
For us a guiding light
That points to workers' liberty,
Can teach us how to fight.
Through good and ill continue still

The Cause that thrives unseen,
That brought the bourgeois tyrants down
In Nineteen Seventeen!

This goes to the tune of John Kells Ingram's "Ninety Eight."

Murder on a London street

Giuseppe's grey head lies where flowing blood
Gives it a glass-black glistening halo, bright
Against the flagstone in the London night;
Thin, old, Giuseppe slumps, exuding blood;
Knee-raised pieta, with no Mary to brood
That startled eyes glitter without sight,
Broken, like a stone-shattered street side light,
Or weep that he lies dying on the road.
Two savage boys, mad with greed, eager
To be enterprising, callous to get on
Met him by chance in the dark, going home alone
And broke his skull; and blood's wage here is meagre!
How much? One hundred pounds his killers took;
I found him dying, bewildered in blood and puke.

James Connolly

(Phrases in italics are James Connolly's)

Young nightsoil man who shovels human shit
Left in the streets for such as you to lift,
Half-starved *Hiberno-Scot* untouchable
Who sign yourself in print *"R. Ascal",*
Here in the crumbling "Labour Chronicle"
Of Edinburgh and Leith, I find your tracks:
A young man's anger stains the page like blood;
A thoughtful, humorous, bitter, loving man,
In hasty, driven, sometimes muddled work,
Still rages, jokes, is fervent — *Hope, and fight!*
A full free happy life for all, or none!

Rage, for a father's useless, broken bones,
For childhood in a noxious Scottish slum,
For children robbed of life and bred to serve,
For women, *"slaves of slaves",* wage-slave or whore:
Rebellion, deep, relentless, righteous, stern,
Not personal alone, but broader, deeper
Sharper, and so unsatisfiable:
You will not thrive, abandoning your own!
The taste and feel of slavery in your mouth,
The need and hope of socialism in your mind:
"A full, free, happy life for all, or none!"
War to the knife, the knife up to the hilt!
You nerve yourself to fight our servile wars.

You say: *We only want the earth!* Freedom
For every *rascal* who must root for hire,

In service with *the slave lords of our age*;
You seek a different world, another Age:
A full free happy life, for all, or none!

Implacable, you carve to shape the future,
Knowing *The only true prophets are those*
Who carve out the future they announce:
Snatch schooling, books, a starveling child with food,
By reason learn to bind unlettered men,
With complex, probing talk unbind raw minds,
Teach slaves to *contemplate their slavery*,
To see their world, remake themselves, to grow;
In action seek to find out how we win;
Help Larkin rouse the helots of the town,
Fight Martin Murphy, the gombeen's* master soul;
Write much and well; help build two mighty unions;*
With Larkin, drill a workers' army; then try
The odds against the old: and, losing, die
Still blazing clean defiance at our foes:
War to the knife, the knife up to the hilt!

But me, I know what happened after the soldiers
Blew you, wounded, half healed, out of the chair,
For an officer to shoot you through the head:
Confronting our descendants of your foes,
I see the things you saw and fought still rampant;
We face Murphy's progeny now, though better tooled
For your example, Spailpin Fanach*, wage-slaves still,
Still driven by *the slave lords of our age*,
As far from your red goal as you: unfree.
A full free happy life for all, or none!

And what did you achieve? You told the court

The will of even your poor few to rise
Proved England's rule a transient usurpation:
A rising, crushed, proved Ireland would be free!
What you said for Keir Hardie fits you too:
Grown up out of the mud in stony cracks
You proved by growing we will rule ourselves,
That bourgeois rule is now and will be ever
The robber's rule, uneasy and usurped!
War to the knife, the knife up to the hilt!
Down through a hundred years your war goes on!
Across a hundred years, I know your voice
Across a hundred years I feel your rage
Across a hundred years, I take your hope
Across a century, I hear your cry
Echo down the years: — *Hope and Fight!*
A full free happy life for all, or for none!

* James Connolly was an organiser for the Industrial Workers of the World, the IWW, in the USA; and then for the Irish Transport and General Workers' Union, founded by Jim Larkin in 1908.

* A gombeen is a huckstering, money-lending petty bourgeois on the make.

* Spailpin Fanach: an itinerant agricultural labourer; a disreputable fellow, a ne'er-do-well. James Connolly signed some of his articles in *The Workers' Republic* Spailpin Fanach.

Lament for David O'Connell

"Ireland without her people means nothing to me" — James Connolly

"They think they have pacified Ireland... They think that they have
foreseen everything, think that they have provided against everything;
but the fools, the fools, the fools! they have left us our Fenian dead,
and while Ireland holds these graves, Ireland un-free shall never be at
peace" — Patrick Pearse

Six hundred years of strife behind,
Of conflict, slaughter, sept and sect;
And Tone* said, we needs must grow blind
To creed and race, for self-respect.
But History spawns on rancid need
Malign sly ghosts who mesmerise
With hate and hope; who plead, mislead,
And, pleading, seed in subtle lies:
Two peoples yet, not citizens, peers,
Still Talbot's** children, William's heirs*.

Saviours in-bred on poisoned soil,
Souls shaped to a Fenian shout,
Minds rough-hewn in turmoil, toil,
Meeting, ambush, camp, redoubt,
And civil, fratricidal war,
Unleashed in Tone's and Emmett's name,
By ardour tender as a roar,
And love impervious to blame:
They wandered blind, by Murder led,
Calling Tone — Tyrconnell came instead!

To finish what Wolfe Tone began,
They masked the face in England's blame

Of Irish folk, and aimed the gun:
Republican name, communal game!
Old watchwords changed, old hopes recast,
"Unity" sunk to sect war cry,
The Rights of Man defined by blast
Of bomb and gun — sectarian lie!
Two peoples fight to hold, regain,
Two songs with one hate-loud refrain.

They'd knock down walls, let in the light;
A mystic's war would malice drain,
Fresh blood and magic would unite
Hate-scarred tribes mad with disdain!
The fools, the fools! Demented choices:
Known history disowned, misread —
Talk to yourself in pantomime voices
And think to hear the Fenian dead!
Can Erin unite, blood-soldered stones,
Despite her peoples, trampling their bones?

* The Ancient Order of Hibernians is a Catholic equivalent of the
Orange Order. It controlled the Home Rule Party before and during
the First World War. Republican contemporaries such as Patrick
Pearse, in the IRB paper *Irish Freedom*, blamed the AOH as much as
— and sometimes more than — the Orange Order for the sectarian
polarisation that led to the Partition of Ireland. Its sectarian-ethnic
account of Irish history dominated thinking and teaching in the 26
Counties for many decades after independence.

*Richard Talbot, Duke of Tyrconnell, was the Catholic leader in the
wars at the end of the 17th century, William of Orange the Protestant
king, victor of the decisive battles at the Boyne and Aughrim. Both
strove for sectional victory. When at the time of the French Revolution
Wolfe Tone, the founder of Irish republicanism, proclaimed the goal
of uniting the people of Ireland "Protestant, Catholic and Dissenter",
he tried to break with that sectional past.

Lament for fallen comrades

Call back the dead! My hero friends of old
Who fled their place in our unequal war
And sank in private life; those who grew cold
To our endeavour, chilled by grief or fear,
Too old to bear, at twenty-five, or nine,
The forceful cutting winds that howl along
Our promontory, anxious to realign
With brutish wage-slave masters seeming strong.
"But Trotsky led to Stalin!" Self-effacement!
No fine disinterested search for truth
But stricken-hearted knowing self-abasement
Beside the poisoned tree still bearing fruit.
Soul wrecked, they make their peace, poor contrite
    braves:
They praise the masters, they who cried "Free the slaves!"

A Hymn to the Godless

(After listening to a recording of poems by Gerard Manley Hopkins)
Once, God and Kate Ni Houlihan were one.
I know Truth, life cleansing Truth, as drought,
Old prayers I'd known, mere talking to myself,
Whimperings in the dark. The priests lied.

And still the sternly sifting natural magic
Of living, ageing, ceasing, dying, fills
Tenuous life with dread and with dismay
At inexorable final cutting down:

Dead folk on leave in the one Elysium,
Time speck that grapples with eternity,
Mind, that will, in time, cease to think,
Roiling sub-mind that will lose all self-recall,
Awareness, aware it rots into oblivion,
Feeling, that will cease to feel, to know,
Seeing, that one day will no longer see,
Sentience, drowning in the Almighty Dark;
Alone, adrift in pitiless space,
Limed in Time's rough blood-bespattered wind,
Feeling, knowing, baffled, yearning, alive,
We bide, and wait for Light and Time to stop.

We dream, drink from the opium-pot of ages,
Breed sly enslaving priests, secrete dim lies,
Spin dialects of sheltering denial,
Break knowing into segments, blind, discrete,
Rig crass tat-markets in parodic gods,
Astrology, tarotry — occult dross:
Cocaine for the people! Fond old tales of God,

Man-made in man's own image, doppelgänger
Of a human-kind that does not know itself.

What can they know who go out fearing, hoping,
Who booze their lives in meek delirium,
Who dare not look out into Time and Space
And know what it says to us of what we are?
There is no other life, no other Elysium,
Nothing, whatever you might like to think,
Beyond a brief encampment at Death's brink.

Everything wears away, will cease to be,
Too soon my time is done and I am gone;
Life, an ice floe in a warming sea
On a world that will crash into the sun!

To face reality with seeing eyes,
To fix with lucid gaze encroaching Night,
To dare to know where it is you are, and what,
To live within the maw of Death and sure
Annihilation, and not fall to Despair
Or self-betrayed dehumanizing lies;
To walk, always alone, stalked by Death,
And not be overawed or Death-infected,
Or spend life dreaming of an afterlife,
Or make, by a single hour, a premature
Surrender to Death's hypnotizing power;
To build within intrinsically blind
Meaningless lives expanding human meaning,
Beyond mere pitch of light, although you know
That there is not, nor can there be, ever,
More than short staring back with life-lighted eyes
Into lowering, all-sufficing, endless night.

And the rising after Easter?

"And I'll be seeing Papa soon, please God"
Wrote Patrick Pearse, before they shot him dead,
Leave-taking from his mother; "We, please God,
Will be together in a while", he added,
Flinging Faith against oblivion: near it.
The last into the pit at Asquith's feast,
"Into thy hands Lord I commend my spirit",
Poor Casement by the rope said after the priest.
These pioneers could think themselves well-set,
That there would be for them a happy ending:
Rebels with a celestial safety net
And credit in God's bank, theirs for the spending.
We must be braver, now Death lasts forever.
You pay for light: you die when you wax clever.

Too long a sacrifice

My mother hated "rocks" and classical music.
"Rocks", she called big words: had she a name
For music? That I cannot now reclaim;
But I picture her angry grimace-quick
Moves to kill an offending radio,
As close to spitting as an angry cat
Made edgy, challenged in her lair by "Dat
Aul nize!", as if pursued by an ancient foe.
She, who loved the Irish music; told
To us her own-made tales of magic geese,
Fairies, giants, ghosts, and fantasies
Of Devils called to dance who kicked up gold:
A lev'lling Bakun'-manqué** mind, my mother's :
Too long a skivvy for shoneening* others.

* Aping "your betters". Shoneen means "little John", signifying "little
John Bull", someone aping English and Anglo-Irish genteel upper
class ways — for example: calling a bonham a "piglet"; a dire insult!

** Michael Bakunin, one of the founders of anarchism.

Demands with menaces

Come here! The harassed mother slaps the child,
To stop the little savage running wild;
Stay there! The boss and his cop soon tell the man,
Who was the child trained so since life began;
Lie still! They tell the girl, and then the woman:
Biology and gold make you half human!

Accept! His social world will tell the prole;
Avoid more pain and grief: stick to your role;
Don't buck iniquity you can't hope to solve,
His instincts tell him then: don't fret, don't delve.

Don't hope! Solidarity won't save your soul:
Make the best of yours, forget the whole!
Don't see the meanness in the ruling clans,
Don't ask why they should rule, don't thwart their plans;
Don't fight for something fine, in a world they've soiled;
Believe what you are told, be reconciled.

Stay there! The harassed father tells the child,
And slaps the little savage running wild:
Stay there! The slap backs what he says,
And they'll slap you into line through all your days.

The Voyage of Vladimir Columbus

"And tomorrow I sail far away
O'er the raging foam,
For to seek a home
On the shores of Amerikaiy".
(19th century Irish song)

"O my America! my new-found-land"
(John Donne, To His Mistris Going To Bed)

Bold Vladimir Columbus sets his sails due West
Into the stormy deep unknown, much-charted seas
To find Amerikaiy: he goes at last to quest
For the Unfound Land. Where others hide and bide, he'll
    seize

The chance; for he is sure his crew could, sailing to Hell,
Prevail, they who have learned their trade in harsh rough
    schools:
Map-makers have well done their work — practice will
    tell
The true mariners from the prattling tim'rous fools

Who haunt the shore, and dream of a far-off unfound
    Strand,
Loath to launch their craft out on the raging main,
Though they too know the next New World is now at
    hand
And can be won— chains to break, a world to gain!

Vladimir knows this tide may go again and strand

Them there becalmed on shore, dim dupes to passive
  hopes.
With straining sails and bodies stretched and torn, his
  band
Of heroes fight the waves and tides until the ropes

Have strands of flesh clinging to them, the waves are
  blushed
In red of their own blood, and myriad dead float thickly
Out on that bitter deep Sargasso Sea; 'til hushed
In awe, they reach Amerikaiy, logically

Where they want it to be. And yet, it is terrain
Unknown, uncharted, nigh undreamed about, they've
  found.
There Vladimir unfurls, 'midst lightning, sleet, hail, rain,
His proud, no-quarter flag on icy, volcanic ground.

Amerikaiy, the quested-for, the unfound land?
Vladimir knows: "Here is no Amaerikaiy!"
He dies aghast, not sure what land it is. Brigand
Liar Josef, knows: " Amerikaiy, I say!".

II
A savage wild dark place — Reversed Atlantis, rearing
Unmapped, in far stark sea, askance the old, gross world,
Athwart the new! Lost, they dream of realms of sharing;
Hurled back, they think they've set the future to unfurl

In untilled land, less free of brute Necessity
Than older worlds; where Want, which withers human
  life
Is sharper, harsher, deeper, stronger; where no City

Of God can build amidst the depredating strife

And endless war — all against all! Wars fought for place,
Or freedom; wars to stay on top, sweet nature's heir,
Or rise; wars of the Lords of Life, mankind's disgrace,
To hold their vanquished slaves — class war, raw and
    bare;

A place of bondage free of mercy as of laws,
Where those who fight serf-making Josef, Vladimir's
    friends,
Are branded warriors in slavery's foul cause;
And all that strives, resists, mad Nero-Josef rends.

New waves of Death engulf them now; the land is
    flushed,
Swamped in drained red blood; the dead are piled up
    high,
Deep as the bitter sad Sargasso Sea, 'til, hushed
In awe and fear, they bend to Josef's Enthroned Lie,

And hail the Liar King their God: "Behold our Sun!"
He, who curbs free act and thought with the butcher's
    knife
And State-Empowered Ignorance, who turns the gun
On Spartacus, and Kepler too, in distraint of life!

Some of Vladimir's friends defy the tyrant's roar,
And live: they vow Vladimir's song still they'll sing;
Bivouac; build anew by the cold volcanic shore;
Raise clean sails, and go to sea once more; seeking.

III
And so, the fierce Odysseyan heroes who outfaced
Rude Nature fell. They left a land inside a shroud
Of blood — Josef's "Amaerica": there he disgraced
The Quest, redrew the maps, purloined Vladimir's proud

Red Flag for the ruin wherein he peonised and maimed.
And we stand stranded on the shore, perplexed lost band,
Our own Amerikaiy unknown, unseen, unclaimed,
Chained to bleak Necessity's iron countermand.

Many who went to Josef, because our world is foul
Turned back in grief, hating the false and savage place,
"Amerikaiy", that was no Amerikaiy. They growl,
And curse those who quest still: "A mad, malicious race!

"No world can live without the slave and king brigand;
No new Amerikaiy is hidden in the sea;
There's no escape from cold Necessity's command
Amerikaiy will never be!" — tired fools decree.

And yet, Amerikaiy does loom for humankind,
Will rise, new Indies, in the wild free furious sea;
And in no far-off place — nearer than that, they'll find:
It will rise up in our now calm, familiar sea!

And we will climb from Necessity, mankind trepanned,
To Freedom: dwell in Amerikaiy ; find the way
To make a world with neither slave nor ruling brigand,
Our own long-sought, long battled-for Amerikaiy!

O my Amaerikaiy! My Un-Found-land.

I learn to tell the time

Winter light waning, window behind us,
We sit, becalmed, crouched by the turf-fired grate,
Elbows on knees, our palms spread to the heat,
Talking: her sleep is heavy all around us.
Hard times: she has gone back again to serve
In the workhouse hospital for seven nights
A week. Two kids, snatched sleep, too many fights;
She can not last for long, nor can his nerve.
Our time was nearly gone; and there, he took
It in his head to teach me to unlock,
To "read", the secret signs on our old clock
(I never would teach him to read a book).
For years we measured time after he went
By the ticking of the money-wires he sent.

Apologia

Should I one day run into Trotsky,
I think I'd shake like a child:
How could I look him in the eye,
That eye so far from mild?

Like Tommy coming home again,
He'd ask me what I'd done
And what could I say to placate him?
"I did my best, Old Man" — ?

And could I tell the stark flat truth:
I did the best I could,
Weighed down by me, a timid youth,
Ignorant as aul King Lud;

That I joined his routed army, beneath
Its flag of inconsequence:
Joined a remnant mad as death,
That I hack my way toward sense?

So yes, if I one day met Trotsky
I'd blush like the child I began;
But then I'd say, that eye on me:
"*I will do my best*, Old Man!"

The curse of Trotsky

Two things I cursed are gone out of the world.

De Valera's sealed green Catholic arcadia,
Small frail redoubt of revenant Gaels: epigones
Mocking the past in a foreign tongue, faith-maddened
    pride
— Green shawls, gold kilts and all-devouring clerisy,
Peasants and priests against "the filthy modern tide"!
On the rocks from which they cast raw millions on the
    sea.

One thing I cursed is gone out of the world.

Cain-Stalin's closed, plague-stricken, ghost-infested land,
Dead at the core; burlesquing class society,
Awash with lies, all forgery and contraband;
A continent afloat in a lapping sea of blood,
As savage as old Muscovy or Samarkand:
A mutant horror in the place where Hope had stood

Two things I cursed are gone out of the world.

Alas, that curses have more force than fond desire:
Look what succeeds to rule by commissar and friar!

The blue rose of forgetfulness

An anonymous "young Labour MP" told Radio 4's "Today" programme that the "Red Flag" should be rewritten as the "Red Rose."

"The historical memory of the bourgeoisie is in the traditions of its rule, in the country's institutions and laws, in the cumulative art of government. The memory of the working class is in its party: the reform party is the party of poor memory." — Leon Trotsky.

Tune: The Red Flag

The Kinnock* Rose is blooming now
In Thatcher's shadow trained to grow:
It signifies apostasy,
But circumstances change, you see.

So raise Neil Kinnock's standard high,
Old principles we'll sell and buy,
Though Reds may flinch and trotskies sneer,
Chameleon politics rule here!

His love was like a red, red rose,
But disappointment changes those
Who have the sense to learn from life,
Now Kinnock plies the traitor's knife

All capitalists he used to hate,
But Kinnock changed, and not too late,
He's seen the truth, the market's tops,
Those without bread can eat the slops.

Hot words were lightly spoken, Neil,
But mind must bring the heart to heel,
One must grow up and take one's stand
With those who wield power in this land.

With values covered, swear we now,
To circumstances we will bow,
The homeless can grow stiff and cold
The sick will thrive when they have gold.

A rose by any other name
Is still itself, remains the same,
The climate shifts, but we stay true:
Dear Margaret, we will ape you!

The Kinnock Rose is blooming now,
In Thatcher's garden trained to grow,
And 'ere young Ramsay Kinnock's through
This rose he'll tint to duck-egg blue.

So raise Neil Kinnock's standard high,
Old principles he'll sell and buy,
Though Reds may flinch and trotskies sneer,
Chameleon politics rule here!

* Neil Kinnock was leader of the Labour Party from 1983 to 1992.
Initially on the left of the Party, he shifted Labour to the right and
prepared the way for the neo-Thatcherite coup in the Labour Party led
by Tony Blair and Gordon Brown after 1994.

We fight the sea at Kronstadt

Across the frozen, hostile, misted sea
To Kronstadt, to attack entrenched White Guards
Manning the garrison there, mysteriously
All-powerful, where once we could command,
Talking now to our own as we talked before:
Workers' control, soviet power (with no
Bolsheviks!), peasant rights — echoing the roar
From the countryside: impossible demands!

What could we do? Abandon the fort commanding
Petrograd? Call it off? Surrender? Give up
The workers' power, looming chaos notwithstanding?
No: we would take a stronger, firmer grip,
And fight to bridle History run amok!

We marched to conquer fortress Kronstadt;
Beating them as we beat the other Whites
(Who did not sound like us) wreaked bloody spite.

We marched to conquer Fortress Kronstadt:
Under their guns across the ice-clad sea
Went Congress delegate and soldier elite;
Their cannon smashed the ice on which we stood;
The abyss opened under us; ice closed
Above white-sheathed warriors splashed with blood:
The ghostly camouflage, pale cloaks like clouds
We wore, did duty too for billowing shrouds.

After, when our bodies were reclaimed from the sacrifice,
The red still showed, frozen, in long coffins of ice.

A dying socialist to his son

Their sick old order burgeons, I decline,
"Perspectives" narrowed to a blurred grey line,
Part of nothing big, soon to prevail,
Or, early, thrive: seed-sower, maybe, mail
From a future possibility, perhaps.

What's left? Will, refusing to collapse,
Hate, sustained by the sight of needless pain:
The homeless amidst great wealth, out in the rain,
Huddled, like cattle by a grey stone wall;
Cash-cultured ignorance — lives made small
And narrow, where life might be broad and fine;
Where "ours" in everything bows down to "mine"!

Love, that sees with awe the calm brave eyes
The uncowed and uncorrupted gaze
With which a wanted, cherished child surveys
A too-disordered world, that will reward
The grosser instincts, curb the best, urge toward
Dominion, avarice, false-hearted pride,
Teach love and fellowship to flee and hide.

And Hope, capable of flaring bright and high,
Fostering progeny to challenge the Lie
That rules in the name of truth: class slavery
Decked out in Freedom's purloined finery!

Hope, righteous hate and love that will not die
In this nadir of the cause they all decry;
Hope, for others, and love: for us now — will

To fight life's entrenched tyrants now, until
We've lost the last grim fight, ourselves grown still!

Maura Rua

Did you hear of "Maura Rua" — Red Mary? She
Betrayed her absent husband: Queen, Tyrant,
Red murderess hated by the tenantry
She tortured for the craic, and racked by rent.
Lascivious "Maura Rua" — Godless, shameless
Red haired glutton inside your castle hall;
Young vicious steward to a husband blameless
But for you! Lovers? Taken against some wall...

Legend: therein Clare memory* records
And heightens truth found too in written words:
Wife of a dead Confederate** pistoleer,
She married one of Cromwell's overlords:
In these old helot tales, pure hate inheres,
Outlasting fact, alive three hundred years.

* Most of the stories I heard as a child are dim now, except for how she
met her end. Her avenging husband was coming home and, in a
panic, she fled on horseback. She looked back, perhaps at pursuers,
and didn't duck in time as the speeding horse went under a bridge,
knocking her head off
** The Catholic "Confederation of Kilkenny".

Schoolbooks

We bought schoolbooks in Ennis classrooms then:
Penny by penny the poorest paid. My mother
Would skimp on call; some found it too much bother,
And some could scarce afford to feed the children.
One day my Reader disappeared, and when
The teacher searched the desks was found, covered
In flowery wallpaper. The small thief hovered,
Shamed; blushing and trembling, he was beaten.
And me, I sat and saw him cringe and beg,
A nervous clever granny's boy, an orphan
Of eight or nine, Anthony Cullinan,
Who boasted to me once he'd eaten an egg.
Property has rites, and children's' rights are slim:
I redden still for what we did to him.

Old Trot

Waning unsatisfied, he can not rest,
Can not give up, give in, resign, desist;
Enlisted for long war, will still resist,
Living defeat, will scorn defeat; his best
Is decades back, his place in life a quest
Uncoupled half from hope: stiff clenched old fist,
Shouts, "victory or death!" into the mist!
Long-lived Nestor doing time to attest
For siblings who died young. "No end but death!"
Meant not what it means now when he caught breath
At thrilling certainty, and will whose bequest
Stirs vigour in him still, youth's fixed behest,
And now, as then youth's purposes persist,
And victory or death still echoes in the mist.

Charlie Van Gelderen, the last person alive of those who attended the
founding Conference of the Fourth International in September 1938,
was a Trotskyist for 70 years. He died in 2001.

Mary plays nuns' school

Now, Mary places papers all along the kitchen,
On table, dresser, chairs: small girls at school;
Herself the nun, alone with children in her den.

Mary is re-enacting school, the convent school,
Where little girls are shaped, chastised, cut
By holy women strung alive to God's tight rule.

Now she begins to teach: she stiffens, starts to strut
Facing the girls, like nemesis engaged,
A long thin stick in hand. Slowly she starts to "tut".

"Tut-tut! Tut-tut! Tut-tut!" Soon anger sparks to rage,
Deep-rooted rage: a wounded eye-less Id
Seething with rancid, poisoned life inside a cage.

Now she begins to shout: she scolds her paper kids,
Upbraiding them as fool, dunce, dim-wit:
Ne'er-do-well, bad little sinful Patsies, Neaves and Brids.

From shouting soon to action: now she starts to hit
The table, the dresser, the unfeeling chairs
With the thin stick, face clenched, caught up, reliving it.

She slaps the table, the dresser, slashes at every chair:
Wood rings on nerveless wood, with rapid blows,
In frenzied mimic violence, 'till papers tear.

Mary slashes and beats, her eyes fierce that they glow,
Lost in fevered playing at nuns' school,

At home, in DeValera's Ireland long ago;
Lost in that wounded re-enactment long ago.

A scene I witnessed. Mary, who would have been about nine, was a pupil at the girls' National School, run by the Sisters of Mercy, the only girls' primary school in Ennis. These nuns had a reputation amongst the poor of the town for being very severe and violent with the children, but selectively so. They were relentlessly punitive, physically brutal and persecuting with the "industrial girls", who were in their full-time custody; less severe, though still very severe, with the children of the poor; and noticeably less severe, or not severe at all, with the children of the well-off. That at least was their reputation amongst sections of the poor practising Catholics in Ennis.

After the Dictatorship of the Lie

European Stalinism collapsed in 1989-91, to be replaced not by democratic socialism but by the capitalism of the state-looting oligarchs. The battle sketched in here, between despair and nihilism on one side and, on the other, understanding and the sharp sense of responsibility, was fought out then in the minds of many socialists.

"The lies dished up and spread by the powerful machinery of government... can reach everyone, everywhere... to imprison social consciousness." — Leon Trotsky, 1937.

I pondered all these things, and how men fight and lose the battle, and the thing that they fought for comes about in spite of their defeat, and when it comes turns out not to be what they meant, and other men have to fight for what they meant under another name." -— William Morris, "A Dream of John Ball." *

A. Yes, in the Century of The Lie
The Greater Lies bred kings
And gun-clad Liars ruled.
In the Century of Enthroned Lies
Truth was defamed, un-natured,
Constricted, stifled, stulted.
In the Century of the Lie,
Usurping Lie acclaimed as Truth,
Determined what was true.
And when the seminal, breeding Lie,
Clad in armour, fire-power, myth,
Is in command, then Truth
Alloys with obscurantists,
With priests who pray alone,
Cranks, flat-earthists, loons

Forever out of tune;
Truth blinks, maimed, ugly
In sudden helplessness,
Sovereign by right, overthrown,
Outlawed, hunted, lost,
Hiding, cold in the heather,
Afraid of the showing moon.
Yet, slowly, meanderingly,
Truth does win fast control;
What's gone comes back again;
Though never at your call;
The beaten rise again,
Furled flags again unfurl!

B. No! Don't think that there is
A quirky god nearby
Who hoards a clean discerning
Bank of seeding Truth on loan,
Or think for consolation
That Truth has staying power
To last and claim its own:
Annulled in its own time,
Its seed drawn off, its place
Usurped, its strength unstrung,
Aligning eyes all burned out,
The vanquished banished Truth
Consigned to scorning laughter
Is a bloodless shade thereafter.

A. 'Till strong lies dry, and crack!

B. By then Time has moved on:
There is no going back!

Your Truth will lose its name,
Lose both its sense and shape,
If you let its time escape;
History a rushing river,
You cannot hone your sword,
You will not plant your flag,
By this same stream again:
You cannot steer your craft,
Nor will you fight your fight,
On this same tide twice;
Truth must ride its Time:
There is no going back!
And when the Lie, raw malice spent,
Sinks down on History's tip,
Shy, limping, ghosted, blind old truth
Comes bent and shadow king
To a world the Lie has schooled
And seeded through with lies.
Faint echoed memories remain
Of outcast, banished Truth,
Moult words from off a theory
Whose practice stalled and failed;
Shard-bits off a perspective
That lacked the maps and means;
Shot rags from a philosophy
That could not fill its sails,
Interpreting the world
It tried and failed to shape.

A. You fight the fight and lose,
But then you'll find your cause
Work through, not as you'd choose,
But unexpectedly,

Made strong in long adversity:
Humankind makes its history
And History makes man.
(And you? Do what you can!)

B. Rude History allows
No replay matches:
There is no going back!
Where once the Lie has ruled
Late-truth will not un-sink
What lies have sunk, or prop
What levelling lies have felled,
Un-seed where lies have raped,
Re-group what lies, amok,
Have disarranged and scattered,
Un-shrivel what the Lie,
All overshadowing, shrivelled,
Or rouse our martyred dead!

A. And yet, new generations do
Reclaim defeated Truth,
Fight its fights once more;
And then the Truth you lost
Works its way through:
We make our history,
Though not as we like or at will
History makes, and remakes, us;
The beaten rise again,
The victors fall apart;
Long furled-up flags unfurl;
Know this for our new start!
(And you? Play your proper part!)

B. Lies make no restitution!
The Liar keeps the spoils
His heirs may sell the loot:
Starved Truth, come back, must sign
Acts of Oblivion,
Make peace with the Lie-offshoots.
History does not atone.
Once done, your chance is gone;
The losers die alone,
Beaten, barren, sterile as stone.

A. You fight the fight and lose,
The victors loot and breed,
The beaten fall apart.
And yet, ideas do survive,
Ideas carve new routes;
Long-doldrumed flags fly;
Our cause will yet prevail.
Though mortal men and women die,
Protean Truth revives, thrives.
Transformed, renewed, replenished,
We will rise again!

B. Then ask Leon Trotsky why
Truth fell before the Lie,
And tell dead Trotsky why
This is the Century of the Lie!

A. But we will rise again!

*John Ball, a priest, was a leader of the peasant rebellion in England,
in 1381, in which he lost his life.

Why our flag is red

The "Butcher's Apron", tri-colours galore,
Flags of present might: paltry, passing things!
Our flag, Flag of the proles and of the poor
Denotes long war, and rooted will to fling
Red truth against encumb'ring lies, to try
Our strength — until humankind wins Liberty

Eireannach!*

(After reading Lecky's History of Ireland)

What is it then, the Irishness
Fate laid on me in this largess?
A world I lost I scarcely knew,
The childhood land I never outgrew,
My father's life, my mother's tales
Of hungers, wars, workhouses, jails:
The memories not quite my own,
To which my memories are sewn.
Inextricably in Erin's net,
I am what I want not to forget.

* Irishman.

Collage for a bleak April, I

April 1989

1. Bronterre Manqué

I have spent the splendid years
That the Lord God gave to my youth
In attempting impossible things
Deeming them alone worth the toil
Content to scatter the seed.
— Patrick Pearse

The revolutionary
About to fail and die
Who died and rose
As he had planned
And as he knew he would
Because Jesus had;
Who failed and died and rose
A Fenian phoenix in his time
The spirit of an Ireland he imagined
And shaped posthumously
Achieving strange impossible things,
That may prove yet
To have been impossible.

Go for it man!
There's lots of bread
To be made in Vegas,
And I don't mean tips
But big bucks
If I hook up with the right operation.

— John Travolta

About to fail and live
In a movie on TV
Singing in Hollywoodese
Consoling anthems
Epitomes and fantasies
Of "The American Dream":
Follow the dollar
In the sky,
Hovering,
Like Constantine's high mesmerising gibbet
Above the looting armies
And their supine victims,
Casino optimism for the disinherited
Consent-evoking myth
Self-hypnotising mantra
Metaphysic of democracy and money:
You too will get your turn, be rich
Appropriate labour not your own:
When the celestial slot machine
Throws up three pictures of yourself
You will attain big, big bucks,
Democratically represent great wealth:
The lucre-lubricated pluto-democratic dream
— Go for it man!

And I have spent the years physicians
Confounded nature
To win for me
Following Pearse
On a deeper track
And on a longer darker slower trek

Across the noisy market-places of slavery, dreaming
The socialist dream
— Go for it workers!

Myself
Here in a Peckham pub
Despairing, drunk
Lost in reverie, surprised
That I have lived so long
Grown so unexpectedly old
Done so little:
A doubting tired old priest, greyed
Bronterre washed up in Fleet Street pubs:
Bronterre manqué
With thirty years in a foreign band, banished
Outside of our own time
Seed-bearing emissaries
From an age unborn, unwon,
Precocious tribunes of a future trapped
Smothering in its caul,
Revenant pioneers, striving
To stop the tide that's gone from going out
Unquiet ghosts who look and see
And think and feel,
But cannot touch or move
The heavy circumscribing world;
Mutant remnants of Lenin's broken horde
Squabbling, groping ignorant squatters
On demesne lands overgrown, de-mapped,
In huts and hovels we construct
From ruined edifices,
Stones from broken arches
Anointed with old sanctity: stranded

Between the Appian crucifixion
And the resurrection.

2. The harp that once

The harp that once
The hope that once
— We know the road behind us best —
Consoling hope and daily guide to millions,
The harp that once in Tara's halls
Its soul of music shed
The Hope that once
Is now malignant, jarring open lie,
The grimacing foul festering
Dehumanising scare-the-crow
On totem poles and tanks
Of the predatory tyrants who murdered it,
And in its vanished self, the consolation,
Sharded, irksome, blood-spurting, bitter consolation,
The spur and guide
Of ones and groupuscules:
The harp that once in Tara's halls
The soul of music shed,
Is now as mute on Tara's walls
As if that soul were fled.

Have I spent the years of my youth
Attempting impossible things?
Dependant addict of inverse myths
That parallel and complement the bourgeois tale,
Its mirror and its other self?
Are the years that I have spent
"Hoping and fighting"

Years spent in a waking dream,
My mother's dream disguised:
A world recast
Benign big human family
Well taught by love to reason,
The bitter-tongued obstreperous
Soft-hearted dream
Of human solidarity— ?

Yes, indeed, dreaming!
But is it senseless dreaming?
The compensating self-consoling fantasy
Of a remade world
To serve as aureole in this
False-hearted heartless world,
Booze for the soul
And self-finagling lies for the will,
Religious dreaming,
Intoxicated raucous commie sighing
For a place unlike our own,
In the vale of woe
Where humankind is doomed
To rule by carnivores,
Cartels and schools of predators,
Binge-feeding, gibbering
Self-righteous cannibals
Preying on their kind
Forever — ?
I know the hallowed dream
Of what humankind can be
And I know its opposite, living
In the bowels of its blood-grimed enemy, amidst
The stench and ugliness

And shame
Of a tawdry tinsel-rich imbecile-minded
Endless mockery of what might be
Of what humankind could — at will! — construct:
Until I die
I'll let that vision,
Sweet aisling in a poisoned world,
And my own old notion of what I am,
What I,
The taste of slavery in my mouth,
Must be, inspire me,
Spur me, shape and reshape me,
To fight for it, live for it
If needs be die for it!

3. The need to know

And yet! And yet
Faintheartedness must have his due:
I want to know. Is it
Mere self-consoling myth we cultivate?
Is it a dream that died
And must remain forever dead,
Echoes and flashes
From battles fought too long ago
That never can be fought again:
Remnant of an era vanished, gone
Never to be called back, lost
In History's shimmering shifting vistas
Where possibility and mirage mix and merge,
And vanish,
Sometimes to reappear:
Is it a dead dream mouldering unlaid

Or seminal new-world-encoding seed?

I do not know
I cannot know
No one can know:
Predestination's lost his maps
Determinism's in two minds
Teleology still seeks God:—
I do not know:
There is no knowing in advance.

Even Plekhanov did not know:
How can anyone believe
He is chosen by history?
That is possible only
With the past.
In the present it is senseless:
Only braggarts and swindlers
Can look at themselves
Through such flattering spectacles.

There is no knowing in advance;
No one can know: — I
Must stand my ground
Hold myself in my place
Unsure of what I am, knowing
That I may never know,
That maybe only others will
From what I help grow.

Collage for a bleak April, II
4. What Is To Be Done?

Trotsky knew:
I see the bright green strip of grass
Beneath the wall.
And the clear blue sky
Above the wall
And sunlight everywhere
Life is beautiful
Let the future generations cleanse it
Of all evil, oppression
And violence
And enjoy it to the full.

Zbigniew knew:
Go upright among those
Who are on their knees:
Let your anger be like the sea
Whenever you hear the voice
Of the insulted
And beaten.

Marti knew:
With the poor people of the earth
I want to share my fate.

Connolly knew:
Impartiality as between
The strong and the weak
Is the virtue of the slave.

Marx knew, *Engels* knew:
History is the history
Of class struggles
That each time ended
Either in a revolutionary
Reconstitution of society, or
In the common ruin
Of the contending classes.

Rosa knew:
The proletarian revolution
Is at the same time
The death knell
For all servitude
And oppression.

Rosa knew:
When the working class
Seizes the entire power
Of the state
In its calloused fist
And uses it
To smash the head
Of the ruling classes,
That alone is Democracy,
That alone is not
A betrayal of the people.

Trotsky knew:
A party or a class that rises up
Against every abominable action
Wherever it has occurred,
As vigorously and unhesitatingly

As a living organism reacts
To protect its eyes
When they are threatened
— Such a party or class is sound at heart.

Connolly knew:
Contemned and despised though he be
Yet, the rebellious docker
Is the sign and symbol to all
That an imperfect civilisation cannot last
For slavery cannot survive
The awakened intelligence of the slave.

Connolly knew:
To increase the intelligence of the slave
To sow broadcast the seeds
Of that intelligence
That they may take root
And ripen into revolt;
To be the interpreters
Of that revolt, and finally
To help in guiding it to victory
Is the mission we set before ourselves.

Gramsci knew:
Reality is the result
Of the application of wills
To the society of things:
To put aside
Every voluntary effort
And calculate only
The intervention of other wills
Is to mutilate reality itself.

Lenin knew:
To say that socialists cannot
Divert from its path
The labour movement created
By the material elements
And material environment
Whose interaction creates
A certain type of labour movement
And defines its path
Is to ignore the truth
That consciousness participates
In this interaction and creation:
With Catholic labour movements
 It was the consciousness of priests
And not the consciousness of Marxists
That participated.

Trotsky knew:
Face reality squarely;
Do not seek
The line of least resistance;
Call things by their right names;
Speak the truth
No matter how bitter it may be;
Do not fear obstacles.

Connolly knew:
The only true prophets are those
Who carve out the future they announce.

Trotsky knew:
Be true in little things
As in big ones;

Steer by the logic of the class struggle
Be bold
When the hour for action arrives.

Trotsky knew:
Tell the truth.

Lenin knew:
It is necessary to find
The particular link in the chain
Which must be grasped
With all one's strength
In order to keep the whole chain in place
And prepare to move on
Resolutely to the next link.

Gramsci knew:
The emancipation of the proletariat is not
A labour of small account
And of little men; only he
Who can keep his heart strong
And his will as sharp as a sword
When the general disillusion is at its worst
Can be regarded as a fighter
For the working class
Or called a revolutionary.

Tsintsadze knew:
Woe to him who cannot wait!

Zbigniew knew:
Let your sister scorn
Not leave you;

Be courageous,
Whenever the mind fails you,
Be courageous:
Only that is important.

Tsintsadze knew:
Many others too have died
As I am dying,
In prison or internal Exile:
It will enrich our tradition;
A new generation, learning
From our struggle
Will know
On whose side truth lies.

Marx knew:
The knell
Of capitalist
Private property
Sounds.

Marx knew:
The integument is burst asunder:
The expropriators are expropriated.

Gramsci knew:
Only the one who wills something strongly
Can identify the elements
Which are necessary
To the realisation of his will.

Cannon knew:
The thing that inspires life,

That makes life worth the living
In face of all the dangers,
Uncertainties
Insecurities
Calamities
Disappointments,
Is to have committed one's own self
To the effort to change it.

Pearse knew:
It is not sufficient to say, I believe,
Unless one can also say, I serve

Rolland knew:
Pessimism of the intellect,
Optimism of the will!

Pearse knew:
Did ye think to conquer the people
Or that law is stronger than life
And than our desire to be free?
We will try it out with you,
Ye that have harried and held,
Ye that have bullied and bribed,
Tyrants, hypocrites, liars!

Connolly knew:
Hope, and fight!

* Aisling is Irish for "vision": an aisling is a "vision poem".

Stalin's legacy

Utopia strait science had become:
Blind capital itself carved out our way,
Trained our army, happily was dumb:—
No chance they'd win sweet History's delay
Or Nature's pardon! We would gain sure sway,
Sweep Gold aside: the workers could assume
Control of social property, loom
Red nemesis; avert bourgeois decay.
And now? Old labour movements fall apart,
And Socialism consists of sects, some mad
Folk who hail feudal Islam's crazy jihad;
Reactionaries: poor as at the start.
From science to Utopia once more?
Utopia lies dead there on the floor!

Their reason and ours

And what is reason but sums, cold calculation
About fixed things? Be reasonable! Don't doubt;
That sums are sure, strait as strangulation:
Know life is flat and static. Do not shout
Against good sums, or kick against computers.
If Freedom is necessity, bow down!
The sum sets mind-ruled man in gear, neuters
Fond hope, desire, fine fantasy, brands clown
The heretic who says, "This is insane,
This tyranny of the bourgeoisie's abacus!"
Life's richer than the counting houses of Cain,
Or Kepler's mind, stronger than Spartacus:
Be brave against their lie, pace subtler drums
And hold your course: subvert, augment their sums!

Report from a war zone

A. How goes the war?

B. It's burning down, I guess.
In hills and hollows and ancient caves
Inside the half-unknown interior,
Guerrillas still lie lurking,
Probing for weaknesses:
They cut off vital roads,
Sometimes, they paralyse,
Erupting periodically
In unforeseen and unexpected ways;
And still, sometimes, in ways all too familiar,
But they do not destabilise the state.

A. They too grow old and tired, it seems!

B. Controlling them takes far less energy,
Consumes less time;
They are, I'd say, under control:
I now have time and energy for other things.

A. That's all you can expect,
For they are irrepressible:
Like fleas on a cat, or herpes!

B. Only an atomic bomb, or a speeding car,
Or guerrillas of another sort,
Destroying their world, will wipe them out.

A. Feebler now, but still they lie in ambush?

B. Spies, they have, to tell them where to strike, and
   when!

A. Oh, their timing is remarkable!

B. They strike from hills and hollows
   And from deep ancient caves and cavities
   Inside the half-unknown interior!
   But yes, they, they too, it seems, grow old.

Time Machines

Time flies — but so can I!
I flit, gadfly, pilgrim
Around in time; I fly
Back and forth at whim,
Zoom in and out and back
And forth through years, decades
And centuries — through cracks
In the fabrics of Time, afraid
Of nothing, guaranteed
Through wars and slaughter, safe;
I go at my own speed
Involved, but calm, aloof:
The safest place to be,
My Time Machine, sweet vale
Of wisdom: all to see,
Time-free, at Colindale.*

*Colindale, in North London, is where the British Library's newspaper depot is
situated.

At the end of history

In our New Age, this Age of Gold,
We've reached the end of History;
All things on earth are bought and sold,
All things, including you and me;
The rich can keep the good green earth,
Now socialism is cause for mirth.

They'll not now blow your world apart,
The bourgeois and the Stalinists
Who have converged to praise the mart:
No longer cramped in Stalin's fist,
New converts see with heady zeal,
This is the better way to steal!

Wage-slavery is here to stay,
Karl Marx and Trotsky got it wrong
It's proved there is no other way
Than plunder by the rich and strong:
"Without it they won't have a job"
Crows Rupert Pig to Captain Bob.

And God's not dead at all, not he,
No matter what some lame-brains say;
He changes form, our Deity
From Age to Age, in his own way:
He dwells now at the Stock Exchange,
Inheres in stocks and shares, like mange.

The Age of Reason never dawned,
We settled for the "Hidden Hand";

And History has never spawned
Its conscious self, to take command:
The working class forever must
Stay down and cringe, mere social dust.

Pre-history will never grow
To socialism, as Marx once taught,
It stops here where sad embers glow,
Where freedom still is sold and bought.
If you can't buy it — tough! Like me,
You're trapped in bourgeois liberty.

Mass culture too was all my eye!
Who needs it in this Golden Age?
We have *The Sun* and pigs can fly
For *Sport,* now Kylie is front page;
And civilisation spirals high
When millions worship Princess Di.

Old Chartist notions came to nought,
Year-Parliaments are not OK!
The bourgeoisie was never caught,
They never gave control away:
But still we vote: "democracy",
Anointing good wage-slavery

You've got it good now, here unfree,
The chains are padded here below:
Though tyrants rule in industry,
We've got what freedom Trade allows:
That's all that you can hope to see,
Here, at the end of History.

Revolt would lead us to new Gulags,
You cannot doubt that was the root
Dried blood turned brown the too-Red Flag,
Of tumult and revolt the fruit!
They knew it would, and long before:
That's why they crushed and robbed the poor.

A jackboot stepping on a face
Forever, Orwell said is how
History stops and sets in place;
But Orwell got it wrong, for now
We keep the Right and plight of Man
To rob his neighbour if he can.

The starvelings now will never rise,
Hungry ideals cease to live,
The rich will always take the prize;
All against all, and never give:
No Age of Solidarity,
Just you for you and me for me.

City of God? Megalopolis!
Utopia? A clicking till!
From rural to urban idiocy
We have advanced, and advance still:
The working class will never rise:
Class war is peace, and truth is lies!

I dreamt I walked with history

A. I dreamt I walked with History
Along sure paths already set and mapped;
I marched with confidence and courage, critical
But loyal and dependable.

B. I followed my sweet mist-enshrouded mirage
Until it stopped,
And there beneath its shimmering heart I found
A dark nocturnal cavern, deep and wide,
Filled up top high with human bones and skulls,
Beneath the foetid, foetal ruins.

A. I, who dreamed I walked down known, sure paths
With History,
Travelling triumphantly,
Inexorably,
The reservations made,
Down payments paid,
Safe-conducts guaranteed,
The destination sure and set,
Must now begin again!
Now I, vicarious power gone,
No Socialist Fatherland intact, not one,
I must go, if I go,
Since History's lost her wits,
Into the cold unmapped unknown!
Alone, along a steep and rocky road!

B. Pathfinding pioneer,

Camp follower no more!
I must walk with guilt and with uncertainty,
And play Poor Tom to mad, blind, wayward History.
Thus disabused, I reach my age of reason,
Know myself for what I am,
Attain my own full height at last:
Self-guided, I must cut new paths to other hills,
And there help build
Tangible, clean, real things.

A. Not me. Not me! — I'm off!

The destiny of lambs

"The Lord is my shepherd;
I shall not want!"
The Lord is thy shepherd?
He shall not want!

Discussion pieces

"I cannot see how that can be",
I said, with winning charm;
"I cant see why you can't see!"
He lied; so I broke his arm

Roots

Cockney in voice, English by birth
And domicile, he hears, one apart,
The teacher's cool, cold dissertation,
Recalling Erin's Great Starvation
Matters of fact, no call to fret,
(The telly shows you worse than that).
"Hunger in England, in forty-five".
A young lad says, "They had to grieve
For we came first; Got some relief".
Teacher replies: "Meal, not beef..."

Alone, suddenly under threat,
The anger tightening in his throat,
He hears, knowing our Famine tale,
With stomach tense, breath quick, face pale;
His hurt grey eyes are raw nerve ends
Extending back and down, wound
Root-tight to starved and murdered folk,
Beyond sea, years, past callow talk,
Tied by our memory to those who died.
"That's me you're talking of!" he cried.

Our Lady of the Jungle Sings the Blues

Mrs. Thatcher Advises Cameron and Clegg on Tory Social Philosophy

With the foresight of genius, Margaret Thatcher offered guidance to
Cameron and Clegg, and to "Tories in the coming time", 23 years ago.

*After the first of her fifty-three standing ovations
subsides, Mrs Thatcher speaks to the audience and the
TV cameras*

Never-ending war of all against all,
The law of the raw jungle since the Fall,
That is humanity's highest moral code
The code of our fathers in true blue woad:
You do to others what they might
Do to you. There is no respite:
Be sure you do it first.
The weak and defeated are the truly cursed.
"Woe to the vanquished," the Roman said,
For, my friends, in the long run we are all dead!

Freedom? The true freedom
The law of God's own kingdom
Is the freedom to sell and buy
The freedom to try or die
And the God-given freedom to prey,
Ruled by a government which says, "OK",
And 'anything goes' to its friends,

Your means are justified by the end,
By your goal of getting rich.
Nineteenth century Liberal kitsch?
But that true freedom, my friend,
Is the only proper human end
And necessarily it partakes
Of the raw blue jungle, and wakes
And tears for the failures and for those
On whose gnawed bones the victors rose.

The health of our jungle-bred species
Is paramount — it hurts, but here's my thesis:
To be poor now you must be a louse.
The weak to the wall and the poor to the workhouse!
The weak to the wall, or none of us can survive.
For God tells us we must serve or thrive,
Rise or fall, be hammer or anvil, axe or block,
In this life you must be either knocked, or knock.
You must, my friend, choose: be crunched or crunch.
And Reagan tells me there is no such thing as a free
    lunch!

Trade unions plot and they conspire: they combine
The rabble and the feeble against me and mine.
They gang up the weak to pull down the strong,
And they do most bitter, bitter wrong
To the lords of the jungle.
In office, Labour bungles and stumbles.
Oppressors and tyrants,
They are perverse servants of the weed,
Red spoilers who would stifle the rich
By curbing their life-giving greed.

The welfare state too, stifles
The wholesome jungle. It rifles
The coffers of the rich and of society,
Impoverishing the strong to give a moiety
To the feeble. It's a conspiracy of the weak
Against nature. Soft hearts weep when the poor squeak.
"Poor, poor creatures", they say — but it's snaring
And false: pity soon palls, money is hard-wearing.

Now she becomes dreamy and starts to sing:

"Hush little baby, don't you cry,
You know your mamma was born to die,
All my trials, Lord, will soon be over,
If life were a thing that money could buy,
You know the rich would live and the poor would die."

Now she jerks back to reality: her voice hardens and
becomes strident:

"And why shouldn't it be? Why not?
Why should the rich let themselves be caught
By the Grim Reaper when they might pay
Their way past his toll gate and stay
Alive, to do good work? That's what I
Want to know! So? You can't pay? You can die!
Let wimps say what wet wimps say
(I hear it works so well in the USA.)"

Now she talks in a deeper jazzy voice, half singing her
words again:

"Poppa may have,

Momma may have,
But God bless the child
That's got his own."

Again she jerks back to reality, and again her voice
hardens and becomes high and strident:

"And it's just tough luck
On the brat who hasn't! Why should I give a fuck?

Mercy? Mercy? Well, as Freddy Shakespeare
Put it long ago — the rich see it clear -
The quality of mercy is always strained:
It comes hard, reluctant, pained.
Noblesse Oblige? A reactionary wimp!
Nothing but a bleeding-hearted pimp
Serving and flattering the feeble and the cruds
With his effeminate dos and don'ts and shoulds
To rein in the rich. This is class war!
And we are the press, the cops, the judges and the law.

Our social philosophy? From each
According to our need — that's it, and let 'em screech!
Do we need her in a job or not?
Does he answer to a need we've got?
Or is she just unmarketable waste?
That's the question — answer it to taste.
To each? To each according to what he
Inherits or can get by work or preying. Be free!
Under the law all are equal, but in wealth,
Like health, some get more equal by work, luck or
    stealth.
The great George Orwell explained that long ago, you

see
To the Tory conference back in Nineteen-o-three

Democracy? You've had it! A five yearly ballot
Is so much better, than rule by the bullet.
Every five years or so I'll let you decide
Which friends of the jungle's lords you'll abide,
Like the King's friends of old, to rule over you,
On behalf of Life's enthroned lords. What else should I
    do?

Our future will be secure if we mix
The spirit of the huckster's shop with raw jungle tricks.
You know, I think we could call the TV show:
The 'Little Shop in the Rain Forest' — Let's go!"

Socialist Organiser, 1988

Remote as Spartacus

Remote as Spartacus, his name rings out
Like the rebel shout that died then in his mouth:
Trotsky! With Lenin, he helped faltering
Masses of ardent working-class rebels
Attain a steady will and mind: without it
They might have missed their chance to rise and rout
The bourgeoisie – to seize the power, rifles
In hand – and lost themselves in paltering.
Remote as Spartacus, his name rings out
Like the rebel shout that died there in his mouth.

King of all beasts

No other creature, none,
Can do what we can;
No other species, not one,
Systematically preys
On Man, but man.

The bells of St Mary's

The nun is being banished by her priest
For her own good; he will not tell her why:
She must not know. (And now I start to cry,
There in the dark). She has to leave, at least
For now, in silence, knowing not their guilt
Who ache for her to stay, but must not say.
(Crying bitterly now, ambushed, at bay,
Smothering in the story, as in a quilt).
Bing Crosby, Ingrid Bergman's ailing nun,
"Bells of Saint Mary's": tawdry arts that sway
Shadows behind the flick'ring shadow play.
Weeping in darkness through that strange re-run
Silence-charged futile tears against the tide
That took the one who had, and had not, died.

A cure for ear-ache

On a Special Day, not any day,
You must wait until St Martin's Day,
And then you get a St Martin's cockerel
And a keen-edged, sharpened knife,
A piece of cloth, not any cloth,
But gauze, and then not any gauze,
But red, blood red fresh-dyed gauze.
You squeeze the screaming, kicking bird
Between your knees, hold him
In place and with the knife lift back
A line of feathers across his neck
And cut into the flesh until
The squawking stops and red blood spurts
Out of the desperate fowl
On to the well-placed waiting gauze.
You let it dry, and ever after
That doubly red
Blood-hallowed cloth will cure ear-ache.
It hardly ever worked for me:
Maybe the ceremony was botched;
Or the pagan-Catholic shaman,
Maybe, was morally unfit,
Unclean; had made a bad confession,
Was in a state of mortal sin.
You never knew; it was hit or miss.
Excuses were as plentiful
As helplessness-bred pishorogues* like this.

*Gross superstitions

The higher barbarism

Barbarians at the gate,
Civilised folk within:
Rabble pull down the great,
Mankind begins again:
That's how it used to be.

Barbarians at the top,
The civiliser's rise
Brought to a needless stop
By people rich and wise:
That's how it is today.

The outcasts drained the swamp,
Built social aqueducts;
The rich on the poor can stomp,
On life charge usufructs;
That's how it is for now.

Our world is upside down,
Out of kilter, out of sense;
God is a witless clown
And Clio* far too dense:
But that won't always be.

We will rise again:
Civilisation yet will win!

* The goddess of History

Syphilis

(After reading Isaac Babel's story "Guy De Maupassant")

De Maupassant died at forty three
Crawling on hands and knees,
Eating his own shit,
His syphilitic brain raddled, shrunk;
Already dead, and gabbling
His fear of death,
He died.

Stumbling and falling
Sentient human beast,
Zek at haulage,
In arctic temperatures,
On scraps and cabbage soup,
Isaac Babel, the unhorsed Cossack Jew,
Died at forty-five.

Past master of the "Genre of silence",
He was destroyed by Stalin,
Whom Trotsky called
The syphilis of the revolution.
He knew,
Disease made conscious of itself,
He knew
That to be audibly silent is
To shout and go on shouting
And shouting, until
You are made to scream out loud in a different key.

Oedipus regrets

Tomorrow he'd be off again to Blighty;
The lonesomeness is on him now: the blush
Of freedom drained, ahead, the train's slow rush
To the boat, and to the gas works over the sea.
He'd walked the town, and talked and talked, been free
With drink, and talked and talked, dressed up in blue-
Suit English affluence; he'd quarrelled too.
With Del'a, maybe, certainly with Minnie.
And now, beside the low-barred fire he lingers,
Crooning: his cracking, tuneless voice is hoarse
With feeling; urging me: "Sing!" Distressed, morose:
Surprised, slow tears come down behind my fingers.
In triumph, Oedipus also knows remorse,
And sometimes loves the one he finds adverse.

Brother Rat

The migrant-lean longtailed pilgrim rat
Retreats down, down, down, down
Inside the ship, down from deck to deck
Before the lifting, excavating gang,
Pitiless, relentless, unstoppable. Down,
Grave-digging down, implacably
They strip away the sheltering cargo,
Boxes, bales and bulky sacks;
Lift off the wooden boards,
Roll steel-clanging cross-beams back,
Peel away deck after deck,
Layer by layer, digging down,
Down. Down, down, he runs,
Inside the ship, down,
Below the water line,
Down, deep down, down
Towards the blank steel wall.
Down, and down they go.
Fleeing, hooking, hoisting,
Until there's nothing left
Inside the deep steel skin
But the terror-stricken trapped
Unreconciled small rat,
Trying to run up, up
The stark steel walls — to fly,
And the nemesisian,
Score-settling, booted,
Steel-hook armed
Assassin gang.

The excavating,
Ravening spent
Years, done and dead
Years ganged-up,
Dead years against
Those living still:
Brute lynch-mob
Mad in pursuit,
Ceaselessly
Hook, shift,
Take away
Year after year;
Hook and hoist,
Flicker-mirage
Your tomorrow
Into yesterday,
Gathering speed,
Digging down
Imperiously,
Murderously
Down, down,
Rapidly down,
Down towards
The narrow,
Narrowing,
Narrowing,
Beleaguered,
Final
Small
Shrinking
Glimm-
ering
Tail-end,

Sliver
Of sent-
ience,
Light
And
Time.

The
Final
Glimm-
ering
Tail-end
Sliver
Of sent-
ience,
Lig-
ht

A
n
d

T
I
m
e
.
.
.

October + 75

I, who was many,
Am now not one,
And less than one.

Noel Babeuf
Came out of jail.
The angry crowds
That thronged the streets,
Fervent, earnest,
Overwhelming crowds,
Remaking all
Their seeding world
Would let them make,
The crowds had gone.

Gracchus Babeuf
Came out of jail
With wondering
Wounded eyes:
Where have they gone?
Where had they gone?
Will they come back?

Will they come back?
And then Babeuf
Went into jail
And the guillotine:
Where had they gone?
Would they come back?
Will they come back?

Buonarotti,
Who was many
And then but one,
And less than one,
Who saved the seed,
Found the answer.

They left footprints
Hard in the rock:
Others have followed
Along in their track.

Will we leave footprints
Hard in the rock?
We carry the seed:
Will others follow
Along, in our track?

Buonarotti,
Who saved the seed,
Knew the answer.

To a friend who died for Ireland

(Peter Graham, 1945-71)

Your bullet-holed young neck was not in view,
Nor tortured flesh, nor rope-burned stiffened wrists:
You looked unpained, a self-possessed young priest
In the coffin; and your beard, I saw, still grew.
Twenty years, Peter — twenty! Mid-life flew
For me, was bullet-stopped for you: earth-kissed
In a Dublin graveyard, rags now wrap your quest.
I'm ageing, grey; you are no longer you.
Twenty years! The North's dim war still hallows the gun;
Against our Red, Orange and Green prevail;
The South, thank God's at peace: you blazed no trail
For chaos, through which nothing new could run.
Ireland, Peter! Fine ideals you sang
To ill-matched deeds, and your you-murd'ring gang.

Press the Button Neil

After Neil Kinnock changed Labour's policy from unilateral nuclear disarmament to support for British nuclear weapons, in 1988, there was much speculation: in an emergency would he press the nuclear button to launch the bombs? What follows owes something to the well-known song about a chimney sweep hanged for burgling his employers, "Sam Hall".

Yeah, I'm Press the Button Neil,
How d'ya feel? Like my spiel?
Yes — I finally came to heel —
I'm for real, I'm for real!
I finally came to heel,
I'm press the button Neil.
Damn your eyes!

Yeah, I understudy Mag
(Hide that flag! Hide that flag!)
I understudy Mag
I'll not gag on this zigzag,
Cos I know it's in the bag,
The Big Job, just like Mag.
Damn her eyes!

The poll-deaf left can squeal,
Let 'em squeal! Watch 'em reel!
The joyous bells will peal
The Party won't repeal,
Judge me by the sequel'
I'm slippery as an eel,
Just hear those Tories squeal.
Yeah, I'm press the button Neil
Damn your eyes!

Yeah, I'm smart, I learn from Mag
(Hide that flag! Dye that rag!).
The left is just a drag,
The Left can only nag,
The soft Left's in the bag,
Damn their eyes!

To me the Left must kneel,
Cease to feel, curb their zeal,
To me the Left must kneel,
That's the deal: how d'ya feel?
Must kneel to Great God Neil,
I'll ameliorate and heal,
In heroic words I'll deal,
Maggie's policies I'll steal,
For office I'm febrile;
Yeah, I'm Press the Button Neil.
Damn your Eyes!

If we lose that left-wing tag
(Hide that flag! Burn that rag!)
With me they won't need Mag
And the Big Job's in the bag!
Downing Street!
— Damn your eyes!

Yeah, I'm Press the Button Neil
And my backbone's made of steel:
A man of firm ideal,
In best principles I deal.
Yeah, my backbone's made of steel,
I'm Press the Button Neil
— Damn your eyes!

Yeah, now I've done for Mag:
She's in the bag — let me brag!
Yeah, I'm Press the Button Neil
— Damn your eyes!

Margaret Barry

A scrawny gaunt young tinker,
With thick black hair and too few teeth,
Street-singing through the fairs for pennies:
Bottom of Ireland's underneath.
But like the wild bird on the wing,
She could sing: how she could sing.

Cloughleigh

I walked on the flag-topped wall.
Hemming the peaceful river,
That sometimes flooded the houses,
Across the road from my
Cloughleigh ancestral hovel,
Unsure of what I'd find,

'Till Jane came to the door,
Small, gaunt-cheeked and eighty,
Friendly, beckoning me
Greeting, loving, anxious,
And Tommy's grinning face
Filled the bedroom window.

A far-off Sunday morning,
I was eight, or less.
No smiled benignity
The drunken night before,
Of snarls, sneers, indignation,
That took him to his Ma's.

Jane greatly feared "the buggy"
That took the unwanted old.
Soon, grown senile, violent,
She was taken in the buggy
To the Workhouse-County Home,
After the boat had taken him.

Cloughleigh is a road, the continuation of Old Mill Street, on the old
edge of Ennis. The hovels — so named, repeatedly, in the reports of
the Clare Medical Officer of Health— were pulled down in 1949.

Introduction to "Confessions of a Tridentine Boy"

With the rise of political Islam, and the migration of people of that faith into the main cities of Europe, religious conflict is now more central to politics in the advanced countries than for a very long time; in international politics, religion is more important than for centuries (unless you want to classify Stalinism as primarily a religion). Yet in our quasi-secular society fervent religion is a great mystery to many, and especially to young people. I grew in a world — small town mid-twentieth century Catholic Ireland — saturated in the Catholic faith, and where its priests ordered and permeated most of our lives.

That Ireland, in the fierce Catholic-nationalism of its first half-century of independence, was arguably the nearest thing to a theocracy, in a Western Europe that also contained Franco's Spain and Salazar's Portugal, both of them under clerical-fascist rule. Irish theocracy operated within the structures of a parliamentary democracy. It had intense mass popular support.

"'Ireland is one huge monastery... At every twist and turn of the day a man is reminded of the affairs of the soul. Thus he meets priests and nuns, he passes by churches and convents; he hears bells ringing for Mass, the Angelus, etc." This picture of mid-twentieth-century Catholic Ireland, in *The Furrow*, journal of the Maynooth Seminary, is close to the truth. Catholicism had been fused by history with our national identity and with an Irish nationalism that had more than a little of religious-political Messianism in it.

In the form of ethnic-sectarian history, Irish Catholics were taught the tremendous story of our people's long ages of captivity in the grip of a relentless heretic enemy, and our struggle against the ruling English state, which served landlords "alien in race and creed", for the liberty to be what we were and wanted to be, what God wanted us to be. The cause of Ireland was the cause of Catholicism; the cause of messianic Catholicism was the cause of Ireland...

From the mid 19th Century, Ireland sent out hordes of missionary priests and nuns to many countries, on the Catholic "Foreign Missions". They were supported at home by propaganda about their work, linked in our minds to the stories we heard in school history about the Dark Age Irish missionaries who "converted pagan Europe", including most of Anglo-Saxon England.

Much that was in the religious forms, ritual and observances of that Catholic world was swept away in the 1960s and 70s by the reforms inaugurated by the Second Vatican Council (1962-5) and in its wake. The people within our old Irish Catholic world would have been amazed at the transformation that has taken place. Now priests have fouled their own nest, forfeited their immunity from criticism, and swim now in a rising tide of child sex scandals.

"Confessions of a Tridentine Boy" is an attempt to conjure up a glimpse of that Catholic world, and of an Ireland dominated by religion and its priests, their values and concerns, , as I experienced it as a child, and to draw a sketch of the state of mind of those who lived in it.

Tridentine here means the Latin Mass, which for decades the Church effectively suppressed. The regulation against the Latin Mass has recently been relaxed. There is a glossary, with notes on Ireland then, after the verse.

Confessions of a Tridentine Boy

(The Pro-Cathedral, Ennis, 1950-53)

"It has been said: 'Ireland is one huge monastery'. In spite of exaggeration [this] correctly emphasizes the fact that religion and the supernatural are a vital element in Irish life. At every twist and turn of the day a man is reminded of the affairs of the soul. Thus he meets priests and nuns, he passes by churches and convents; he hears bells ringing for Mass, the Angelus, etc. — The whole atmosphere is conducive to spirituality." — *The Furrow*, organ of Maynooth College, Ireland's leading seminary, 1954.

White surplice on the long, blood red soutane,
Lieutenant at the Mass — "'Tis the holy b'y"
I am! Blue, scented smoke ascends like a cry:
I swing the chain-held charcoal-firing pan.

The smell of incense, candles, wax and wine;
Lost medals, beads and missals piled in store;
Marble, brocade, brass, flowers; priests galore;
The Life Eternal: Mankind and God entwine.

Infant Jesus, Mother Mary, Joseph — all
Life caught, transfixed, inverted. Let us pray
To Christ The King: sweet Saviour, we are clay!
Help us, migrating, not stray beyond your call.

II
Vengeful God, subversive Satan: desire;
The man-God crucified: Death like a bell!

Self-resurrecting Saviour, Heaven, Hell:
Baptism, sin, Last Judgment, eternal fire!

The Body and Blood of Jesus, bread and wine:
The finite, infinite, Death made a liar;
Pray for the Holy Souls in purging fire;
Faith, Hope, dear God, and Charity, be mine!

The Father, Son and Holy Ghost in one,
Both God and man: self-worship and self murder.
Eternal God, and bone and flesh: Great Herder,
Guide our steps to Heaven, this life done!

Peter, Christ's Vicar, Rock of Popes: priest-rite,
Church, human and Divine: Dogma and yearning;
The sin of Eve and Adam; endless burning:
Mother of God, intercede against the night!

III
The Age of Reason: First Communion Day;
Route maps to Heaven: Confirmation rite,
Cleansing Confession — learn to self-indict.
God comfort us in death's sure disarray!

All powerful Mass-caste: Absolution; nuns;
And Mystery — Three Persons in One God —
Not to be grasped by reason, Faith unshod:
Pray for The North, where heretics have guns.

St Patrick, Bridget, all those gone before;
The Way of the Cross: the Via Dolorosa;
And holy water; Jesus, Gael-named Iosa:
Faith of our fathers, lore of Erin's gore.

Brown scapulars, Miraculous Medals; cold
Communion, kneeling; bright uplifted grail,
In spite of fire, jail, sword: praise the Gael,
God's blessed, old, indomitable fold!

Pray that God's own people will endure:
For God and Ireland! Faith and Fatherland,
Where Iosa, Lord of Hosts is in command:
Gallows, Mass rocks, Christ's conquering allure.

Carnations, lilies; Blood upon The Cross:
Good Friday — kiss the Blessed Wounds of Christ!
Midnight Mass at Christmas; all life a quest
For Grace: the crucified God repairs your loss.

Retreats and Confraternities: a misty
Sea of flame, candle in every hand,
Renouncing Satan's "works and pomps", we stand:
Counting gleaned candles in the Sacristy.

The smell of incense, candles, wax and wine;
Lost medals, beads and missals piled in store;
Marble, brocade, brass, flowers; priests galore;
The Life Eternal: Mankind and God entwine!

IV
Four Sunday Masses, sleepy-eyed from bed;
Face-slapping priests; shoe-fights in the sacristy;
Adeste Fidelis: march at Corpus Christi;
Marriages, funerals, Masses for the dead.

In Nomine Patri; church-Latin at eight:
Proud hucksters' sons, and farmers', mis-plac'd prole

(A token two of us from National School);
Children, help priests to Transubstantiate.

Town ladies fixing flowers; counting poor
Folks' pennies; winter mornings in the dark;
Bishop like God; Brennan, the kind cowed Clerk;
De Regge, choir master: organ music's soar.

I chanted answers to the priest by rote
In long-set Latin words half understood;
Helped priests to dress as antique Romans would:
Rites old and set, fixed as in creosote.

I clanged the bell, not always timed on call;
Lifted the lectern-held ornate great Book
Across the altar: backwards, down you took
The steps, then up (too small, I let it fall!).

I held the silvered paten out to seize
And save our God, made bread, should He slide out
And down from some poor palsied, broken mouth:
I saw blind Dev there, cower on his knees.

The smell of incense, candles, wax and wine;
Lost medals, beads and missals piled in store;
Marble, brocade, brass, flowers; priests galore;
The Life Eternal: Mankind and God entwine!

V
Vengeful God, subversive Satan: desire;
The man-God crucified: Death like a bell!
Self-resurrecting Saviour, Heaven, Hell:
Baptism, Last Judgment — sin: eternal fire!

Peter, God's Vicar, Rock of Popes: Church-rite
To Die, or Live, by: Dogma, Tradition, yearning;
The Heritage of Sin — and endless burning:
Mother of God, intercede against the night!

The smell of incense, candles, wax and wine;
Lost medals, beads and missals piled in store;
Marble, brocade, brass, flowers; priests galore;
The Life Eternal: Mankind and God entwine!

White surplice to the long blood-red soutane,
Lieutenants at the Mass — "'Tis the holy b'ys",
We were! Dark masking smoke, cascading lies:
I swung the chain-held incense-firing pan.

Notes to "Confessions of a Tridentine Boy"

SURPLICE/ SOUTANE — An altar boy wore black canvas shoes, a light ankle-length red cassock, buttoned at the centre to the neck, a soutane, and over it, to below the waist, a white smock, the surplice, usually trimmed with lace.

MASS/TRANSUBSTANTIATION — In the Mass, the priest changes bread and wine into the "Body and Blood of Jesus Christ". Though to human senses nothing has changed, belief that after the priest has performed the rites the bread and wine really is the body and blood of Christ, "The Real Presence", not a mere symbol of it, is central to Catholicism. Transubstantiation is the core activity in the Mass; only the priest can perform this miracle.

LIEUTENANT AT THE MASS — Altar-boy, server, acolyte. A "server" made responses to the priest as he said Mass. Boy, man or other priest, the responses of the server were an essential part of the Mass, substituting for the congregation. Women played no part, except as congregation. Women could not go into the chapel without covering their heads; men, not without uncovering theirs. (There were women choristers.)

THE HOLY "B'Y"/ B'YS" — Altar boys were forbidden to go to such occasions of sin" as the cinema; some, nevertheless, did. I did, after, at the age of 11, I discovered — by way of Korda's The *Thief of Baghdad* — the wonderful technicolour world that could be visited through the gates of the Gaiety cinema (in O'Connell street, where Dunne's is now). Doing that involved keeping an eye out for anyone you didn't want to see you going in, and when asked either lying or having your face repeatedly slapped. Defiantly going to the pictures inevitably undermined commitment. (On Monday and Tuesday evenings the cinema dispensed with the earliest of its two shows a day, so as not to compete with Benediction at the Pro-Cathedral for the men's Confraternity, at half seven on Monday evenings, and the women's equivalent on Tuesdays.)

THE CHAIN-HELD CHARCOAL-FIRING PAN — A thurible, a small ornate pan on a long chain in which charcoal was fired and at certain parts of the

Mass or Benediction had incense sprinkled on it to produce a strong, sweet-smelling smoke. It would be swung and, the end of the long chain held in one hand and grasped in the other close to the smoking pan, shaken rhythmically a prescribed number of times, billowing the ceremonious smoke.

FOUR SUNDAY MASSES —
Altar-boys were obliged to serve at two of the four Sunday Masses; quite a few of us would serve, from time to time, at four.

MARRIAGES, FUNERALS —
The priests would administer the Sacrament of Marriage, conduct services at funerals, baptise children. A riddle we had summed that up: "He killed his mother, married his sister and buried his father — who was he?" A priest whose mother died in childbirth. The Church controlled education, the state's role limited to that of custodian of "standards". Priests, nuns, Christian Brothers (a monk-like order of celibate teachers) controlled not only the schools but also the orphanages, reformatories, charities, etc.

CORPUS CHRISTI — Mid-year
feast of the Body of Christ and His Real Presence in the Eucharist. In Ennis, after a special Mass, there would be a great triumphal procession through the town led by the Bishop and his priests with statues of Jesus and a consecrated Host, held aloft, at the front. Young women in summer dresses would walk backwards in front of the procession, strewing the petals of flowers on the ground before the Host. All shops were shut, their windows and doorways made into shrines for the day, displaying holy pictures, statues and lots of shrubs and flowers.

THE LIFE ETERNAL — The
belief that each person has a soul that survives bodily death, some to go to Heaven/Paradise and some, those who die in a state of mortal sin, to burn in the fires of Hell for all eternity. There were two other places to which the souls of human beings might go after death, both, so to speak, transit camps to Heaven: Purgatory, which had fires like Hell, where you burned, but only for a time; and Limbo, a place without fire or punishment, but cut off from the joy of God's presence until the Last Judgement. In Catholicism, as distinct from some types of Protestantism and Islam, your celestial fate is not determined

before you are born. What you do or fail to do in life will determine whether in the afterlife you go to Paradise or burn forever in the fires of hell. As our irreverent saying went: "Out of Hell there is no redemption/ When you go there, you set your pension!"

HOLY SOULS IN PURGING FIRE/ MASSES FOR THE DEAD
— Those who die in a state of "venial" (minor) sin go to the Hell-like fires of Purgatory for a certain time. Prayers and Masses said for the dead and Indulgences granted by the Church, can shorten their time — and your own — there. The "working assumption" was that everyone, or most of us, anyway, would do time in Purgatory.
People would pray fervently for loved ones dead, and others they had known, and have masses said for them (at a smallish fee). The great pity and love, and the dread, that went into concern for the "Poor Holy Souls" burning in the temporary fires of Purgatory disarm mockery, even now. The ghost in Shakespeare's Hamlet conjured up Purgatory as we understood it:
"I am thy father's spirit,
Doomed for a certain term to walk the night,
And for the day confined to fast in fires,

Till the foul crimes done in my days of nature
Are burnt and purged away...
I could a tale unfold whose lightest word
Would harrow up thy soul, freeze thy young blood,
Make thy two eyes like stars start from their spheres"
Hamlet 1.5.9-17

LAST JUDGEMENT — The final reckoning with God at the end of the world, when souls will have their records on earth reviewed and be divided into the saved, who go to Heaven, and those damned to Hell for all eternity. Those in Limbo will then finally be allowed into Heaven.

THE SIN OF EVE AND ADAM
— "Original Sin". With one or two exceptions, all human beings are born in a state of congenital sin inherited from our "First Parents", Eve and Adam, who sinned by disobeying God in the Garden of Eden, eating fruit He had forbidden them to eat. They were banished for it into all the troubles and tribulations of humankind, including death; so are their descendants.

BAPTISM — Infants are baptised to clear them of Original Sin; infants who die unbaptised, like the virtuous people who lived before the Birth of Christ, go to Limbo.

THE AGE OF REASON — Is reached at about the age of seven. The child makes a First confession and has a First Communion. First Communion day is a great milestone in the child's life: thereafter the child is capable of Mortal Sin, and is answerable for it to God.

LEARN TO SELF-INDICT — Before confession the penitent "examines his conscience" for sins of deed or omission. These must be confessed to the priest, from whom, as God's representative, forgiveness must be sought and the soul cleansed of sin before Holy Communion can be received, (that is, before the body and blood of Christ can be ingested). Absolution is conditional on sincere inner repentance and, where possible, the making of restitution. Since God knows your innermost thoughts there is no cheating, no escaping. To make a bad, insincere or incomplete, Confession is itself a mortal sin. The belief that God will know if you cheat or are too soft on yourself encourages strict and severe self-appraisal and self accounting. You, so to speak, have to denounce yourself to a vigilant and severe god, who already knows all about you and your private thoughts and feelings. Combined with the belief that most likely you will "do time" in Purgatory, it sometimes fosters, or helps foster, a sense of inexpiable guilt.

ABSOLUTION — The forgiveness of sin by the priest on behalf of God.

CONFIRMATION RITE — At the age of about 11, in a ceremony conducted by the Bishop, children are "Confirmed", as Catholics in the third Sacrament of Initiation (Baptism, the first, Holy Communion, the second), choosing an additional first name.

SAINTS — Saints are dead human beings known for sure to be in Heaven because prayers addressed to them, asking them to intercede with God, are known, and certified by the Church, to have led to miraculous cures and other wonders.

INFANT JESUS, MOTHER MARY, JOSEPH — The Holy Family, Jesus, Mary and Joseph. Jesus was the Son of God and Mary. Joseph was Mary's earthly husband and Jesus' foster-father. He was a carpenter by trade and is the Patron Saint of workers. People would identify with Joseph the Worker, Mary the Mother; and identify also with favourite saints, whose biographies were known by tradition and kept fresh from Catholic Truth Society booklets, articles in the press on anniversaries and saints' name days, and sermons at Mass or Benediction. The choice of your special saint would have a big element of self-identification, and even of class identity, in it. For instance, my mother, and before that, if I understand it, her mother, identified with Blessed Martin de Pores (now Saint Martin), who, son of a black slave in Latin America 400 years ago, was rejected by his white father and did lowly menial's work. "Blessed Martin" was very popular with many in the town. Statues and framed wall-pictures of him were common. In our house we had both his picture on the wall and his statue in the little altar in the bedroom, in which a small linseed oil lamp in red glass burned continuously; in line with our family cult, I choose "Martin" as my Confirmation name.

FAITH, HOPE AND CHARITY — The three theological great virtues.

FATHER, SON AND HOLY GHOST IN ONE — The doctrine of the Trinity: God has three persons, "God the Father, God the Son and God the Holy Ghost", but nevertheless is one being. A "mystery of religion" which cannot be understood by common reason, but which is dogma — something which you must accept as an act of Faith in the Church. The alternative to acceptance of this and other such "mysteries of religion" is exclusion from the Church for heresy, and, in consequence, damnation in Hell forever; in earlier ages it also meant incurring the earthly punishment of death by fire, being burned at the stake.

PETER, CHRIST'S VICAR, ROCK OF POPES — Christ's chief Apostle, Saint Peter, whose original name was Simon, was the first Pope; all the Popes are his successors, deriving their authority from Christ's words to Peter: "Thou art Peter, and upon this rock I will build my Church". Peter means rock.

MOTHER OF GOD INTERCEDE — Mary, the Virgin Mother of Jesus, was born without Original Sin and at her end was taken up to Heaven alive. She has power to influence her Son on behalf of human beings. The first account I heard of what a Protestant is was my mother's: "Ah, they don't believe in the Blessed Virgin." The dogma — something a Catholic must believe — of the Assumption of Mary alive into heaven was propounded by Pope Pius XII in 1950. It was announced and celebrated, in Ennis as elsewhere, as a major event; my own first encounter with the mutability of Faith and dogma.

VIA DOLOROSA — The "Way of Sorrows", which Christ, carrying his cross, walked on his way to be crucified. The "Stations of the Cross" in fourteen pictures of the stages of the journey, ending with Christ hung up to die, adorn chapel walls. "Making the Stations of the Cross", going from picture to picture praying and thinking again about each incident, is a very common practice.

HOLY WATER — Water blessed by a priest, holy water is held in fonts at chapel doors, and in homes; it is touched to wet the finger tips before making the Sign of the Cross .

MASS ROCKS — In the days of persecution, and for decades after active persecution ceased, before the chapels and cathedrals could be built, Mass was said in the open air, with flat stones, "Mass rocks", serving for an altar. Photos exist of the congregation at such Masses. In Ennis, the Pro-Cathedral was built only in the 1840s, three quarters of a century after aggressive persecution had ceased.

GOOD FRIDAY — The day Christ was crucified. It is "Good Friday" because Christ's self-sacrifice then made it possible for humankind to be absolved of Original Sin. On the third day, on Easter Sunday, Christ rose from the dead. Each Good Friday in the Cathedral a big cross was laid on a cushion at the opened gates of the altar rails, and for the three hours which Christ took to die on the cross at Calvary, devotees filed past and knelt to kiss the wounds, marked in red paint, on the figure of the crucified Christ.

FACE-SLAPPING PRIESTS — Physical abuse of children was the norm then, in schools and in many homes (not in mine) and for offences against discipline an altar boy would have his face repeatedly slapped by Father Quealy, the priest in charge of the servers. The avalanche of sex scandal that has come down on the Irish Catholic clergy in the last two decades raises questions here that I can answer only in terms of my own experience. Overtly sexual molestation I neither experienced nor heard of. The sexual ignorance and "innocence" of that time and place is hard for people now to believe or imagine. In my time as an altar boy, between the age of nine and twelve, I simply did not know the "facts of life". Neither, I'm reasonably sure, did most of the other servers. The fear of the priests we had was fear of being beaten. Even that didn't happen all that often. A while back, looking on the internet at photos in the Clare County Library, I found a group photograph in which only some of the figures had been identified by name. Amongst the unidentified stood the prematurely white haired, slight figure of Fr. Quealy. To my astonishment, I found myself feeling indignation that he had been "forgotten" like that. I finally decided I was still in the grip of a mild form of the "Stockholm Syndrome"!

One of the unexpected things in the town was the public existence of a small coterie of very camp, seemingly gay, men, two of whom I remember by name, Michael Tierney and the small hunch-backed Josie Cronin. You would see them camping it up in the streets and, late in the evening, at street corners. They were there all through my childhood, when I didn't understand about such things; the last time I saw them was (my last visit home for 17 years) in mid-1958, when I did. Some of them made a living selling evening papers on the streets: if they had been unpopular or widely disapproved of, that would not have been possible. Memory suggests that they, or some of them, were popular. An agitating priest or friar could, probably, have driven them out of the town; that did not happen. This in an Ireland in the grip of a brutally repressive sexual puritanism, whose devastations were given the same name by the poet Patrick Kavanagh as the popular term for the murderous potato famine of the 1840s, "The Great Hunger".

I have no explanation. Evidently the townspeople's response to stereotypes they also knew as people was better than their own caricatural image would lead you to expect.

MIDNIGHT MASS AT CHRISTMAS — Mass celebrated at the beginning of Christmas Day, the anniversary of the birth of Christ; a tremendous occasion in Ennis, which everyone except the few Protestants in the town would attend, either at the Friary or the Pro-Cathedral. A moment of great excitement, eagerly awaited, at the Pro-Cathedral, was the singing of Adeste Fidelis (Come All Ye Faithful) by a gifted choirboy.

A MISTY SEA OF FLAME/ RETREATS — Every year there

would be two weeks, one for women and one for men, of fervent nightly preaching by visiting missionary priests. (Retreats, we called them, I think.) They were shadowed in their tour of the parishes by sellers of religious statues, medals, prayer books and other literature . In Ennis, these would put up their tent for two weeks in the grounds at the front of the Pro-Cathedral and set out their wares. The week would end with the packed congregation, each person holding up a lighted candle, answering "We do!" three times in chorus to the question spoken three times by the priest: "Do you renounce the Devil with all his works and pomps?" In my memory, "We do!" in reply to the third questioning was three times repeated: "We do! We do! We do!" The candles would then be quenched and left under the seats in the Cathedral to be collected

and used on the altar in the coming months. We would sort them in the sacristy, separating the slightly darker wax from the cheaper, pure white paraffin-wax candles.

NATIONAL SCHOOL/ CHURCH LATIN AT EIGHT — Most of the

servers, who numbered perhaps 30 in all, came from the Christian Brothers School, only two from the National School, where schooling was set to end at 14. There were none, of course, from the girls' schools. Inevitably there was built in class selection. We were recruited at the school, where volunteers were taught the necessary Latin by an older boy, someone near the age for leaving school and altar-boy service. We grouped at the back of one of the classes once or twice a week, learning as best we could. Most of those who started, dropped out. Finally Fr. Quealy came and tested us, and told two of us, Eddie Mulqueen and me, to get the required server clothes — the boy's family had to buy those — two sets of soutane and surplice, and black canvas shoes, a black draw-string cloth bag to carry them, in and clothes hanger to use in the common wardrobe in the sacristy.

SHOE-FIGHTS IN THE

SACRISTY — The canvas shoes which altar boys wore were handy weapons in the fights that broke out in the sacristy. I was suspended once — being "fired", we called it — after a severe face-slapping, when the priest in charge of the servers, Father Quealy, walked in on me leathering another boy with my shoe! (The leathering was all too often the other way around!) Being "fired" was a frequently used punishment; after a while you would be sent for again.

BRENNAN, THE CLERK — Paddy Brennan was the Clerk, the Sacristan, general manager, of the Pro-Cathedral, under the priests, to whom his manner, in the fashion of the time, was always deferential. He had a helper, Picky Dignan. A small, quiet, good-natured devout man, Brennan was remarkably gentle, kind and tolerant with the altar boys, and, certainly, with me; my father being away in England, he allowed me to adopt him as surrogate. Memory suggests that he had a big clutch of children of his own. I would go and help him and Dignan, who was also a kind, good-natured man, after school. I remember Paddy Brennan with great affection.

THE SILVERED PATEN — Only the priest was then allowed to handle the thin, pure white, stiff lozenge of consecrated unleavened bread, the "Host" into which he had called up "the Body and Blood" of Christ. Those who wanted to Receive would kneel outside the low rails that fenced off the altar and a sizable area surrounding it. The priest would go along the line of communicants on their knees and with their eyes closed and place a Host on each extended tongue. A server would accompany the priest on his repeated rounds of the Altar rail and hold a silver, or silvered, paten — very like a table tennis bat — under the chin of each recipient, to catch the Host, should it fall out of someone's mouth. It never did, in my experience. The Hosts were manufactured by nuns at the Convent of Mercy, where they had a little die machine to cut the lozenges, one at a time, from flat white sheets of the stiff unleavened bread; boys would be sent to fetch a box of them; occasionally you might be daring and eat an unblessed host, as yet only the incipient Body and Blood of Christ.

BLIND DEV — The TD for the Ennis area was Eamon De Valera — "Dev". In his later years he was nearly, and then completely, blind. Even when Taoiseach he would walk through the town, with a small entourage and very little visible fuss, to attend Mass, taking his place amongst the worshippers in the pews.

NOT STRAY BEYOND YOUR CALL — It was recognised that many, indeed most, of the young would leave Ireland, and face the danger that in a less religious environment they might cease to "practise their religious duties", and lapse as Catholics. Amongst the concerns was that they would fall in with the "communist" "Connolly Clubs."

VENGEFUL GOD — The idea we had of God was of a relentlessly vindictive, jealous tyrant, obsessed with regulating even the pettier details of our lives, especially our sexual lives, and forever threatening us with punishment in the afterlife, punishment crazily, out of proportion to anything we might do. (For instance, we couldn't eat meat on Fridays, the day on which He, in one of his personages, was crucified. To do so — so my memory suggests — was only a "venial sin", for which you would not be damned to Hell but would be sent to burn in Purgatory for a spell.) The

attitude to Him drilled into us was the abject, subservience of courtiers and petitioners at the court of an absolute monarch. (It derived, of course, from the long epochs of human history when caesars and kings ruled with irresistible power.) We sang the praises of His "goodness" and "mercy" and "love" of humankind, though in human terms, self-evidently from what we knew, and feared, about Him, He was neither good, nor merciful nor loving. What strikes me most about our mental world then was the addled celestial monarchism of it all: "Christ the King", "Mary Queen of Heaven", "Our Lord", "Our Lady" etc., and how very oddly it sorted with our self-proclaimed democratic republicanism in politics.

SUBVERSIVE SATAN — Satan, the defeated rebel against God in the supernatural world, is now confined to his own kingdom of Hell. From there he intervenes in our natural world to wage an endless guerrilla war on God and on humankind. His great obsession is to lead human souls to break God's laws and thus merit an eternity in the fires of Hell. He tempts, misleads, sows disaffection and foments rebellion and sin against the Lord God, the King of Heaven and earth. His greatest success was in temping Eve, the first woman, who then tempted Adam, the first man, to eat the forbidden fruit in the Garden of Eden. Thereby he provoked God into a retaliation against all mankind that will last until the end of the world. It is Satan who is responsible for all the evil to which humankind is heir, because at his instigation Eve and Adam robbed God's orchard and ate the interdicted apple.

LORE OF ERIN'S GORE —
Telling and retelling the story of the long persecution of Catholics in Ireland at the hands of Protestant English governments and their Irish-Protestant subordinate Irish governments, and of the staunch fidelity of Irish Catholics to the Faith, in spite of fire, sword, jail, gallows and despoliation. Nationalism and Catholicism were for us closely entwined, to the point of being merged in one, a sort of two-pronged religion: the cause of Ireland is the cause of Catholicism; the cause of Catholicism is the cause of Ireland. The discovery that in real Irish history it was not always so, that the Catholic Church instigated and Pope Adrian IV authorised the twelfth-century Anglo-Norman invasion of Ireland, that nineteenth-century bishops denounced the Fenians (leftist Republicans), etc., etc., etc., shattered for some of us — in me at 15 — all trust and confidence in the priests, in their Church, and in what they told us about this world and the next, and about God. It reduced me, like many others, to the condition which Karl Marx avowed, in the passage from which too often only one summary phrase — religion 'is the opium of the people' — is quoted, that critics of religion like himself, by their criticism, aimed to induce: "Religion.. is an inverted consciousness of the world . Religion is... this world['s]... logic in popular form ... its moral sanction, its solemn complement, and its universal basis of consolation and justification... The criticism of religion is in embryo, the criticism of that vale of tears of which religion is the halo. Criticism has plucked the imaginary flowers on the chain not in order that man shall continue to bear that chain without fantasy or consolation, but so that he shall throw off the chain and pluck the living flower. The criticism of religion disillusions man, so that he will think, act, and fashion his reality like a man who has discarded his illusions and regained his senses,

so that he will move around himself as his own true Sun. Religion is only the illusory Sun which revolves around man as long as he does not revolve around himself." — *Contribution to the Critique of Hegel's Philosophy of Right* (1843)

Index of first lines

No other creature, none 102
Now, Mary places papers all along the kitchen 65
On a Special Day, not any day 103
Once, God and Kate Ni Houlihan were one 46
Pinioned by History's revenging lie 26
Politics? Talking out 25
Rattling, clatt'ring, reverberating echoes roar 19
Remember me, and hold you strait within 8
Remote as Spartacus, his name rings out 101
Should I one day run into Trotsky 56
Six hundred years of strife behind 43
Spending our lives in outcasts' work 12
Sverdlov killed the bloody Tsar 11
The Butcher's Apron, tri-colours galore 72
The jetsam with the flotsam off the land 22
The Kinnock Rose is blooming now 58
The Lord is my shepherd 95
The migrant-lean long-tailed pilgrim rat 107
The nun is being banished by her priest 102
Their sick old order burgeons, I decline 61
Time flies — but so can I! 90
Tomorrow he'd be off again to Blighty 106
Trotsky knew 80
Two things I cursed are gone out of the world 57
Utopia strait science had become: 87
Waning unsatisfied, he can not rest 64
We bought schoolbooks in Ennis classrooms then 63
What is it then, the Irishness 72
What world is this, sir? 27
White surplice on the long, blood red soutane 119
Who fears to praise Red Seventeen? 37
Why do you misconstrue my view? 17
Winter light waning, window behind us 55

Yeah, I'm Press the Button Neil 113
Young nightsoil man who shovels human shit 40
Your bullet-holed young neck was not in view 112

Dates

THE TREASON OF THE INTELLECTUALS: 1994. Solidarity 8-8-2002
REMEMBER!: 1994. Solidarity 2010
KARL MARX IN AUGUST: Socialist Organiser 5-9-91
IN ASSISI: 1997
AND WHERE WERE JACOB SVERDLOV'S SONS?: Socialist Organiser 5-9-91
"THE TROTS": 1996
PHOENIX!: Socialist Organiser 1988
LEFT-WING ANTI-SEMITE: Workers' Liberty June 1996
LENIN AND TROTSKY LOST: Workers' Liberty Mar 1999
AN ISLAND FOR CITIZEN PROCUSTES: Socialist Organiser 11-12-92
SUNDAY BEFORE WAR: Socialist Organiser 27-1-91
PRAGUE, NOVEMBER '89: Socialist Organiser 1990
AUL' MILL STREET, ENNIS: Socialist Organiser 21-8-91
AN OLD DOCKER REFLECTS ON HIS FATE: 1988
POLITICS?: 1990
TROTSKY AND TIME: Solidarity 2011
THIS IS DYSTOPIA, LADY!: 2010
MURDER ON A LONDON STREET: 1991
JAMES CONNOLLY: 2004
LAMENT FOR DAVID O'CONNELL: 1994
LAMENT FOR FALLEN COMRADES: Socialist Organiser 11-1-91
AND THE RISING AFTER EASTER? Socialist Organiser July 1994
DEMANDS WITH MENACES: Socialist Organiser 26-3-92
THE VOYAGE OF VLADIMIR COLUMBUS: Socialist Organiser 11-5-89
I LEARN TO TELL THE TIME: 1990
APOLOGIA: Socialist Organiser 28-7-91
THE CURSE OF TROTSKY: 1991
WE FIGHT THE SEA AT KRONSTADT: Socialist Organiser March 1991
A DYING SOCIALIST TO HIS SON: July 1998
MAURA RUA: Socialist Organiser 11-5-94
OLD TROT: Solidarity 11-1-02
SCHOOLBOOKS: Socialist Organiser 1989
MARY PLAYS NUNS' SCHOOL: Socialist Organiser 26-10-1989

AFTER THE DICTATORSHIP OF THE LIE: 1988
WHY OUR FLAG IS RED: Workers' Liberty March 1996
EIREANNACH!: Socialist Organiser, January 1992
COLLAGE FOR A BLEAK APRIL, I: April 1989
COLLAGE FOR A BLEAK APRIL, II: WHAT IS TO BE DONE?: web, 2008
STALIN'S LEGACY: Workers' Liberty 1995, web 2010
THEIR REASON AND OURS: Solidarity 2011
THE END OF HISTORY? Socialist Organiser December 1989
I DREAMT I WALKED WITH HISTORY: Socialist Organiser 1991
ROOTS: Workers' Liberty November 1995
OUR LADY OF THE JUNGLE SINGS THE BLUES: Socialist Organiser October 1988
THE HIGHER BARBARISM: February-March 1993
TO A FRIEND WHO DIED FOR IRELAND: Socialist Organiser 21-8-91
CLOUGHLEIGH: September 2010
CONFESSIONS OF A TRIDENTINE BOY: 1990. Web 2008.